ZAC BROWN BAND
Uncaged

C000049636

CONTENTS

This book was approved by Zac Brown Band

Uncaged CD cover design by Brandon Maldonado, Michael Mason, Kevin Leahy, and Brandon Clark

Transcribed by Jeff Jacobson

Cherry Lane Music Company

Director of Publications/Project Editor: Mark Phillips

ISBN: 978-1-47687-467-8

Visit our website at www.cherrylaneprint.com

ZAC BROWN BAND *Uncaged*

Zac Brown Band may have nine hit singles, two platinum-selling records, and countless dedicated fans, but to hear its members talk, they're just getting warmed up. That's right—after numerous nights in front of packed arenas and amphitheaters, things are just beginning to come together for this accomplished band of brothers, led by one of the most charismatic individuals ever to don a beanie and dominate radio.

The band's latest album, *Uncaged* (Atlantic/Southern Ground)—which debuted at #1 on the *Billboard* 200—is proof positive. The result of a highly collaborative process, it's the sound of a group of versatile musicians jelling into a formidable unit and realizing they're capable of anything their fearless leader happens to dream up, from traditional country ("The Wind") to Caribbean rhythms ("Jump Right In") and even slinky bedroom R&B ("Overnight"). Running roughshod over genre boundaries, and bringing its audience along for the ride, its title is absolutely accurate—this is truly the sound of a band "uncaged."

"I think that we've grown so much over the past few years as individual musicians and as a cohesive unit," observes drummer Chris Fryar. "As a band we have really grown together. And we play really, really well together. That increasing level of maturity really shows up on *Uncaged*."

"We're always trying to push the barrier of our musicianship and I'm proud to say that there is a little bit of something for everyone," adds Brown. "It's your basic country-Southern rock-bluegrass-reggae-jam record."

The addition of percussionist Daniel de los Reyes has helped the band move the groove along. His new bandmates describe de los Reyes—known for performing and recording with Stevie Nicks, Sting, Peter Frampton, and Earth, Wind & Fire, among others—as a consummate professional. "It was really great to have him along," says guitarist/keyboardist Coy Bowles. "Danny's not going to be playing timbales over a bluegrass song. So if he needs to play a shaker all the way through a song, that's what he'll do. He knows when to be aggressive and when to lay back. I think the album has a real cool dynamic because of his sensitivity to all that."

Brown has built a virtual southern Brill Building of songwriting talent, while doing his best to reincarnate the '70s heyday of Capricorn Records through his Southern Ground Artists label, home to the Wood Brothers, Levy Lowrey, Nic Cowan, Sonia Leigh, Blackberry Smoke, and the Wheeler Boys. But that's only part of the story. His Southern Ground banner flies over everything from metalworking to leather goods. In addition to housing offices and rehearsal space, the former industrial warehouse in Atlanta that serves as the company's headquarters also features a full kitchen for "Chef Rusty" Hamlin and his crew, the better to power those much-talked-about "eat and greets" that Brown, a former restaurant owner, hosts for lucky fans.

The most farsighted plans reach beyond the warehouse, to a plot of land south of Atlanta where plans proceed for a nonprofit camp aimed to help kids overcoming behavioral problems, learning disabilities, and disadvantaged backgrounds. Simultaneously, Southern Ground has secured a studio in Nashville for future recording needs. At this point it's safe to say that the Zac Brown Band is more than an act—it's quickly becoming a way of life.

So given all of the creative energy around it, new material has never been a problem for the Zac Brown Band. The band was originally built on the songwriting partnership of Zac Brown and Wyatt Durette. Since then the brain trust has expanded to encompass the artists on the label as well as members of the band. No matter how heavily the band is touring, something is always percolating.

So while there are ten credited songwriters on the 11 tracks composing *Uncaged*, all are individuals within the band's social circle—no "guns for hire" here.

Unlike the band's prior outing, *You Get What You Give*, which grew out of songs that had already been in the band's live set before it entered the studio, *Uncaged* was put together from brand-new material. After booking some downtime, they all retreated to the Appalachian foothills near Dahlonega, Georgia. "It had a very cleansing vibe to it," Fryar recalls. "You get really bad cell service there, which was great. There weren't any distractions. We were able to cut off the outside world and dig into what we wanted to say on this record."

They carried with them some 40 songs, none of which had been fleshed out or arranged for the band, and some of which weren't completely done. The goal of the retreat was to pull out and arrange the right 11 songs.

"It was an intensive workshop," notes bassist John Driskell Hopkins. "We hit the record button any time we had an idea worth keeping. Then we'd change things as we went. And we did that in a great place to build a campfire, cook some food, hang out, and have some fellowship too. I'm amazed that we got so much done in just four or five days."

Then, with producer Keith Stegall (Alan Jackson, George Jones) in tow, the band settled in at Echo Mountain Recording Studio in Asheville, NC, to lay down basic tracks, then took a "working vacation" to Key West, to record vocals at Jimmy Buffett's Shrimpboat Sound. Additional overdubs took place in Atlanta and Nashville.

The result is the most expansive album the Zac Brown Band has ever delivered, where the group's trademark vocal harmonies meet jaw-dropping musicianship in a musical world where genre boundaries are increasingly slippery.

But if you think that's going to mean reduced radio exposure and a shrinking audience, you don't know this band very well—or its audience. "A lot of other artists may choose to sit back and do the same record they did last time, because they don't want to lose those fans," Fryar observes. "But from our perspective, we think those fans deserve the best music we can make. If it's different from the past record that's OK, because it's the best we can do. And they deserve the best. They're paying our bills and feeding our families."

Asked whether the band still feels at home on country radio, Hopkins notes that country radio has grown and evolved just as the band has. "It's Southern radio to me, and I don't think we're doing anything Southern people wouldn't like."

"I love country radio because of the dedication they have given us," De Martini affirms. "When I talk to program directors, they tell me they're happy to play it, but they really have no choice because the fans are crazy about calling in and requesting our music all the time."

The album's two featured guests, Amos Lee and Trombone Shorty, aren't Music Row signifiers in the same way Alan Jackson was on *You Get What You Give*, but Brown says this doesn't mean the band is leaving country music behind. Far from it—lead single "The Wind" is "the most country thing we've ever done," he notes. There is no "master plan," he adds. "We were just getting our buddies to sing with us."

In many ways the Zac Brown Band is an unlikely success story. Bands who cover so much territory tend to become critics' darlings, but not platinum sellers.

"The two things I think that make this band different from anybody else, and the reason why we're here today, is that everybody has an insane work ethic," Bowles observes. "Nobody complains. Everybody plays their asses off, everybody gets on the plane or bus even if they're not feeling well, and tries to do everything to the best of their ability, always. And Zac has this ability to make you believe what he's singing, no matter what. So if we do an R&B tune or a reggae tune, he's totally believable. You believe he's lived 'Highway 20 Ride,' for example. His conviction comes through all those songs."

"One cool thing about Zac is that he loves to include everybody," De Martini adds. "He doesn't really have to have the Zac Brown Band. I think he would be successful just as Zac Brown. But the band adds a lot and takes it to another level. It's one big family with him."

JUMP RIGHT IN

Words and Music by
Zac Brown, Wyatt Durrette
and Jason Mraz

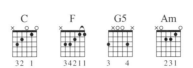

*Gtr. 1: Tune down 1/2 step, capo II:
(low to high) E♭-A♭-D♭-G♭-B♭-E♭
Gtrs. 2 & 3: Tune down 1/2 step:
(low to high) E♭-A♭-D♭-G♭-B♭-E♭

Intro
Moderately slow ♩ = 108

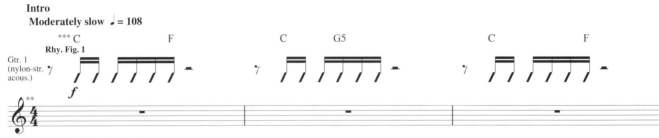

*Equivalent to standard tuning, capo I
**Music for capoed gtr. & vocal sounds 1/2 step higher than indicated due to capo & tuning.
***See top of page for chord diagrams pertaining to rhythm slashes.

The

south - ern wind   sings a - gain an is - land lull - a - by. _____

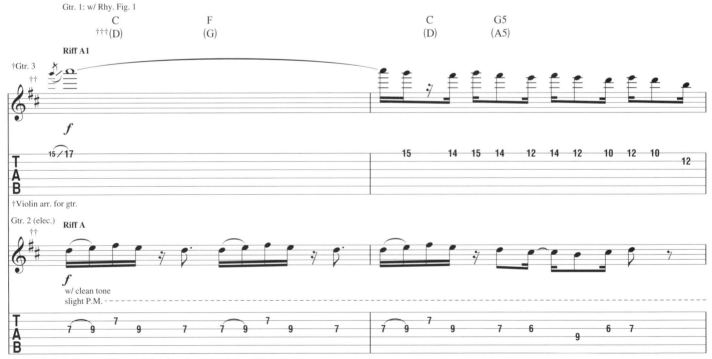

††Music for non-capoed gtrs. sounds 1/2 step lower than indicated due to tuning.
†††Symbols in parentheses represent chord names respective to non-capoed gtrs. Symbols above represent chord names respective to capoed gtr. & vocal.

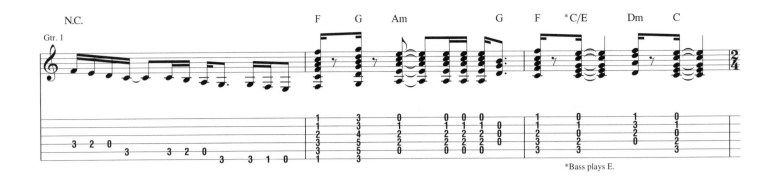

*Bass plays E.

Bridge

You can find me where the mu-sic meets the o-

w/ fingers

**T

**T = Thumb on 6th string

- cean. If you get the no - tion, stop on by

T   T

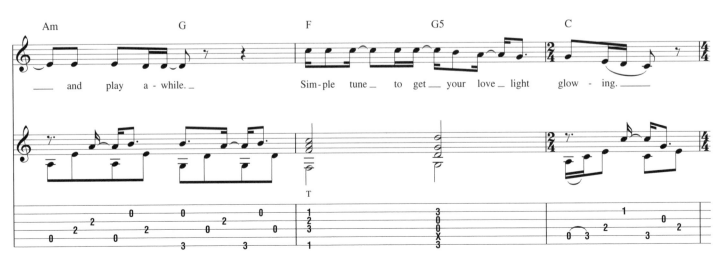

and play a - while. Sim-ple tune to get your love light glow - ing.

T

8

UNCAGED

Words and Music by
Zac Brown, Wyatt Durrette,
John Driskell Hopkins, Jimmy De Martini,
Coy Bowles and Nic Cowan

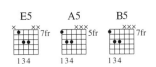

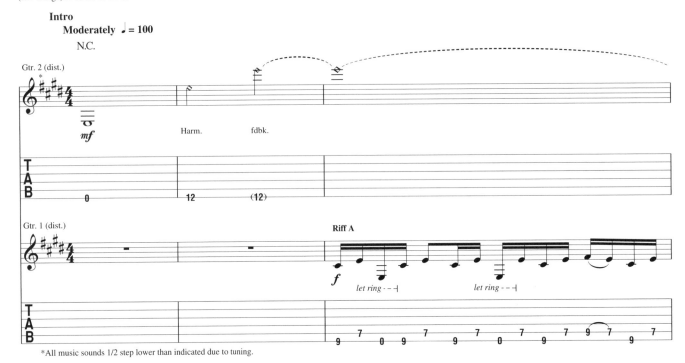

*All music sounds 1/2 step lower than indicated due to tuning.

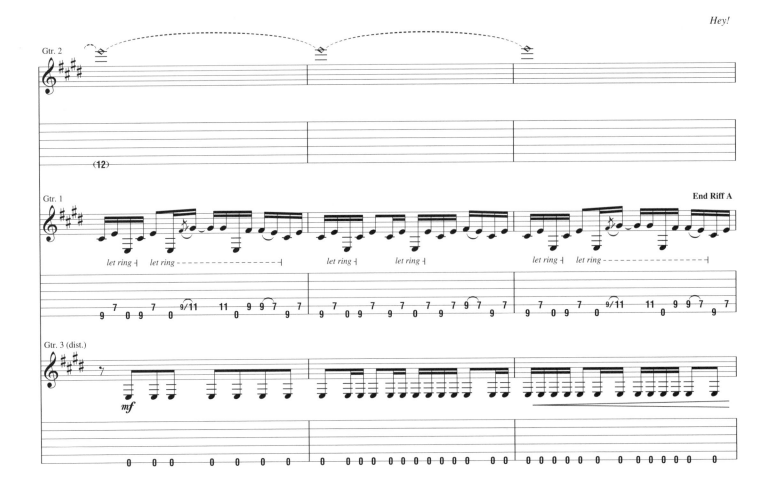

*Chord symbols reflect overall harmony.

**See top of first page of song for chord diagrams pertaining to rhythm slashes.

1. Gon - na drift to the great wide o - pen, ___ gon - na set my spir - it

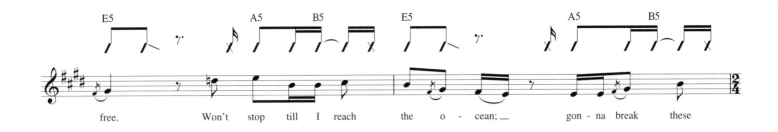

free. Won't stop till I reach the o - cean;___ gon - na break these

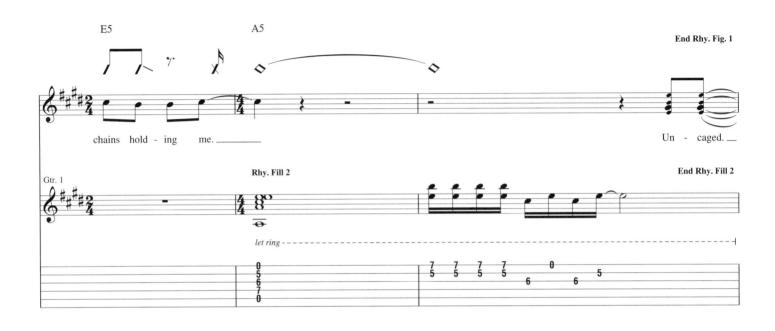

chains hold - ing me.___ Un - caged.___

2. Gon - na swim in the cold - est riv - er,___ gon - na drink from a moun - tain

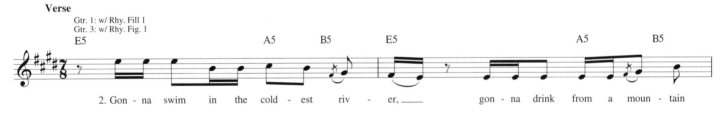

spring. De - fend the land of the great wide o - pen;___ let the wa - ter

roll all o - ver me.___ Un - caged.___

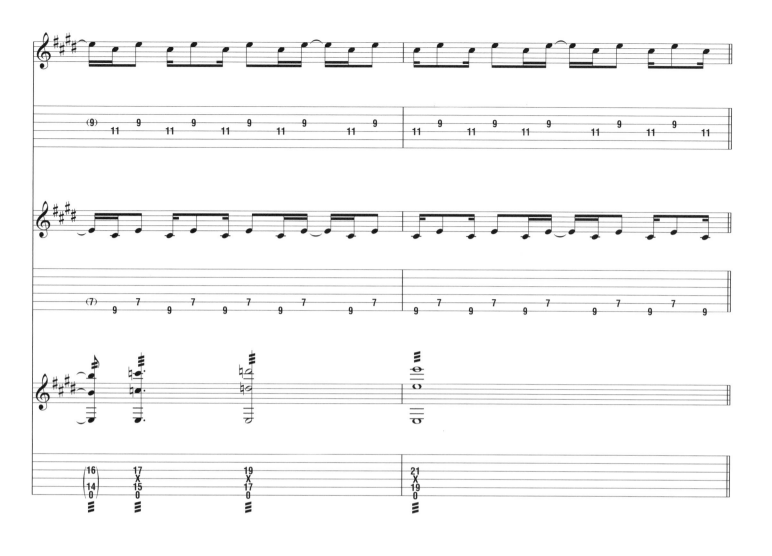

Guitar Solo

Gtrs. 2 & 3 tacet

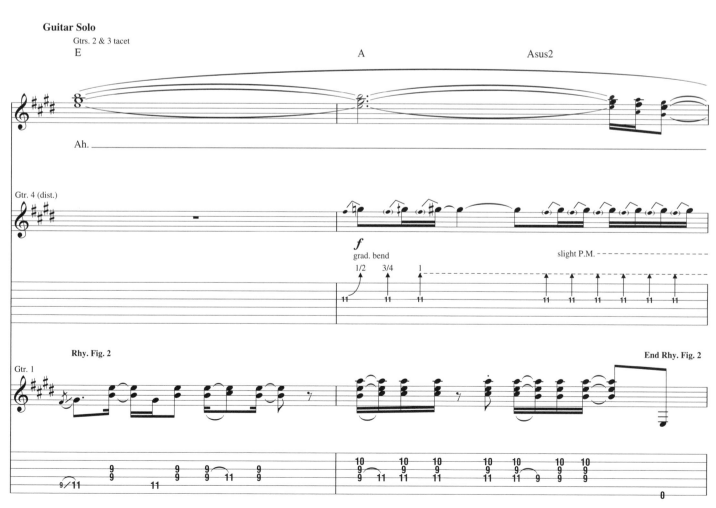

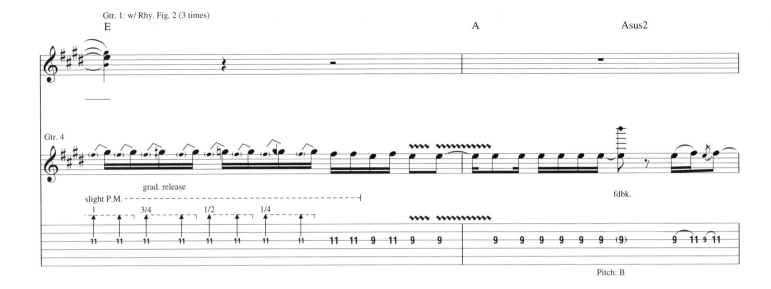

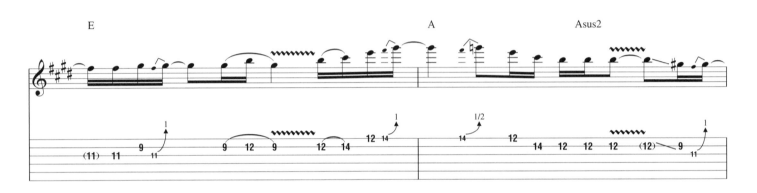

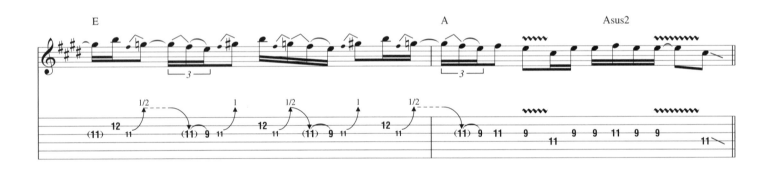

Bridge

I _____ wan - na swim in the sun - shine, _____

*Composite arrangement

ev - er - y day___ find a way___ to face___ my fears.___

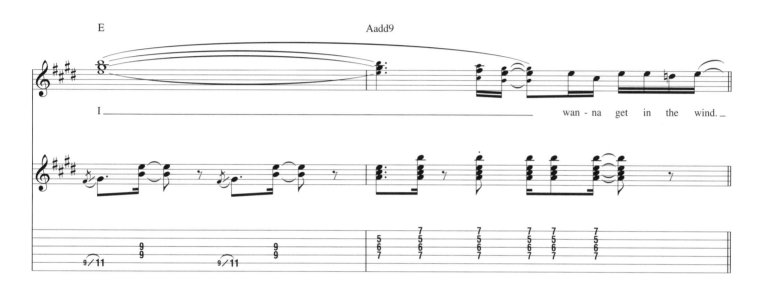

I _____ wan - na get in the wind._

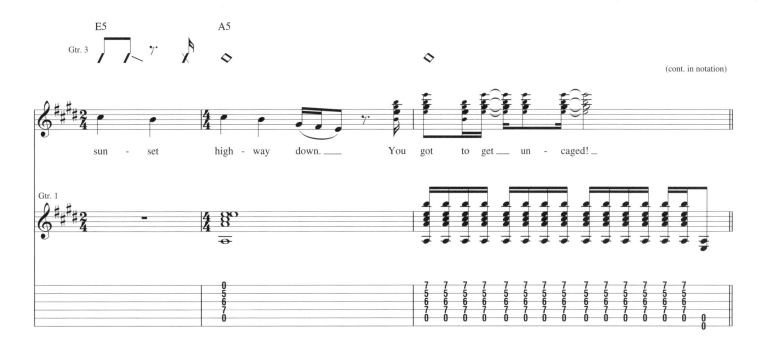

sun - set high - way down.____ You got to get __ un - caged! __

(cont. in notation)

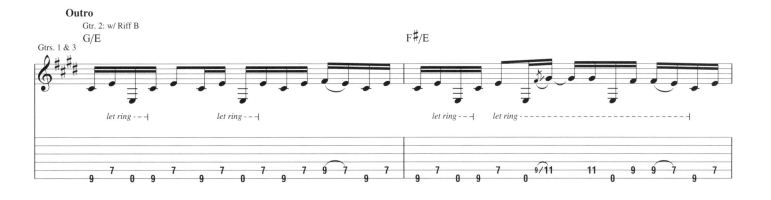

Outro
Gtr. 2: w/ Riff B

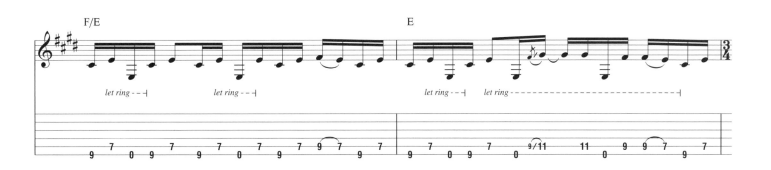

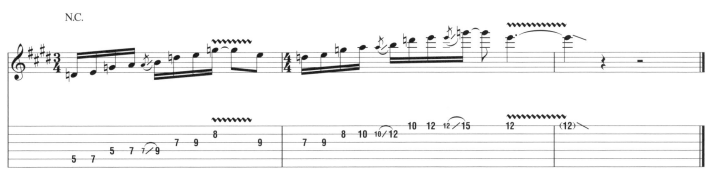

GOODBYE IN HER EYES

Words and Music by
Zac Brown, Wyatt Durrette, Sonia Leigh
and John Driskell Hopkins

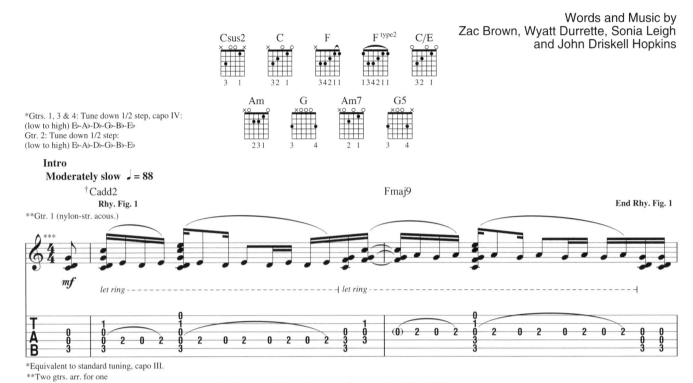

*Gtrs. 1, 3 & 4: Tune down 1/2 step, capo IV:
(low to high) E♭-A♭-D♭-G♭-B♭-E♭
Gtr. 2: Tune down 1/2 step:
(low to high) E♭-A♭-D♭-G♭-B♭-E♭

Intro
Moderately slow ♩ = 88

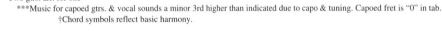

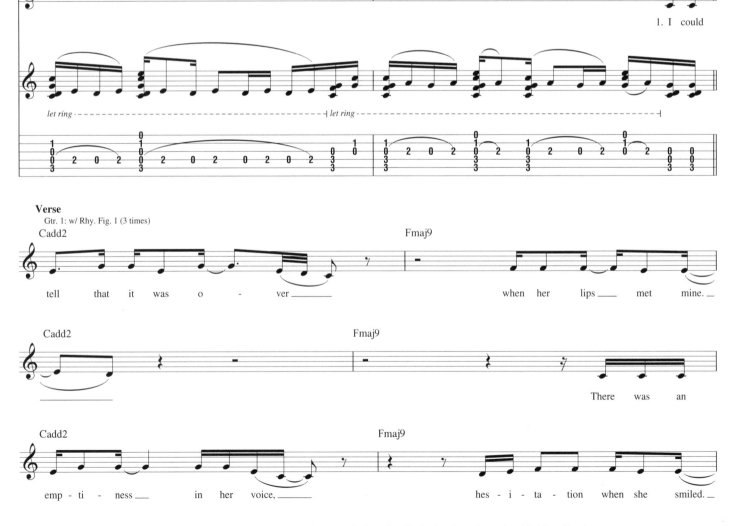

*Equivalent to standard tuning, capo III.
**Two gtrs. arr. for one.
***Music for capoed gtrs. & vocal sounds a minor 3rd higher than indicated due to capo & tuning. Capoed fret is "0" in tab.
†Chord symbols reflect basic harmony.

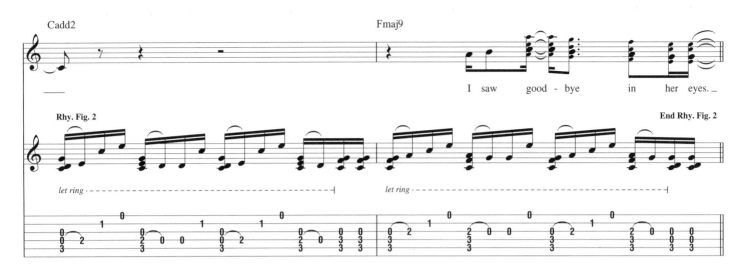

I saw good - bye in her eyes.

Rhy. Fig. 2

End Rhy. Fig. 2

let ring ------- let ring -------

Chorus

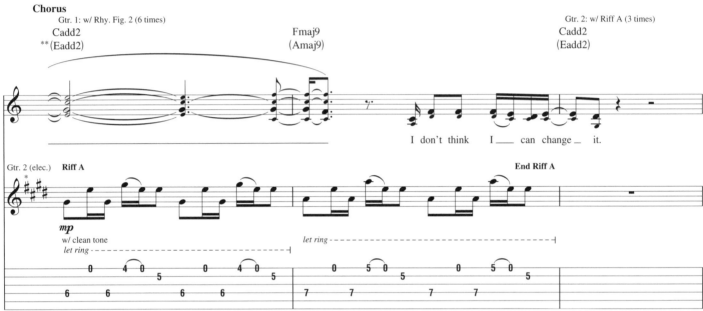

Gtr. 1: w/ Rhy. Fig. 2 (6 times)

Cadd2
**(Eadd2)

Gtr. 2: w/ Riff A (3 times)

Fmaj9
(Amaj9)

Cadd2
(Eadd2)

I don't think I — can change — it.

Gtr. 2 (elec.)   **Riff A**   **End Riff A**

mp
w/ clean tone
let ring ----------------- let ring -----------------

*Music for non-capoed gtr. sounds 1/2 step lower than indicated due to tuning.
**Symbols in parentheses represent chord names respective to non-capoed gtr. Symbols above represent chord names respective to capoed gtrs. & vocal.

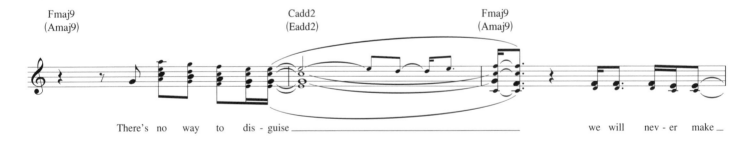

Fmaj9
(Amaj9)

Cadd2
(Eadd2)

Fmaj9
(Amaj9)

There's no way to dis - guise — we will nev - er make —

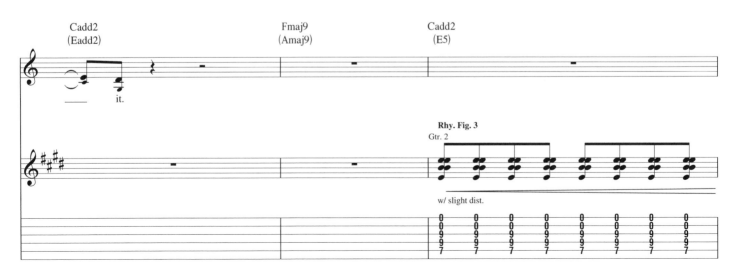

Cadd2
(Eadd2)

Fmaj9
(Amaj9)

Cadd2
(E5)

— it.

Rhy. Fig. 3
Gtr. 2

w/ slight dist.

Verse

Gtr. 1: w/ Rhy. Fig. 2 (6 times)
Gtr. 2: w/ Riff A (6 times)
Gtr. 3 tacet

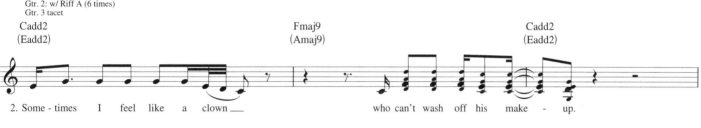

2. Some - times I feel like a clown ___ who can't wash off his make - up.

The life she want - ed, it was gone; ___ Prince Charm - ing I was -

- n't. But I would trade a thou - sand Bab - y - lons ___

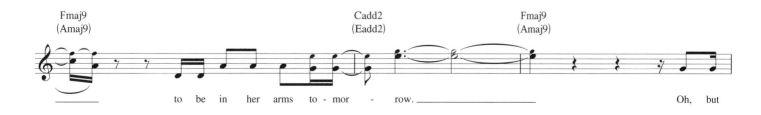

___ to be in her arms to - mor - row. ___ Oh, but

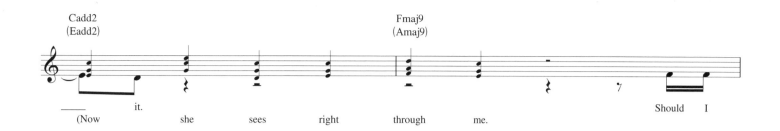

Cadd2
(Eadd2)

Fmaj9
(Amaj9)

it.
(Now she sees right through me.

Should I

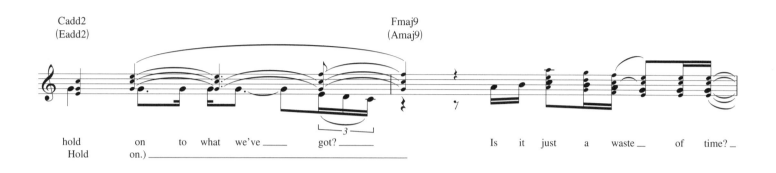

Cadd2
(Eadd2)

Fmaj9
(Amaj9)

hold on to what we've ___ got? ___
Hold on.) _____

Is it just a waste ___ of time? ___

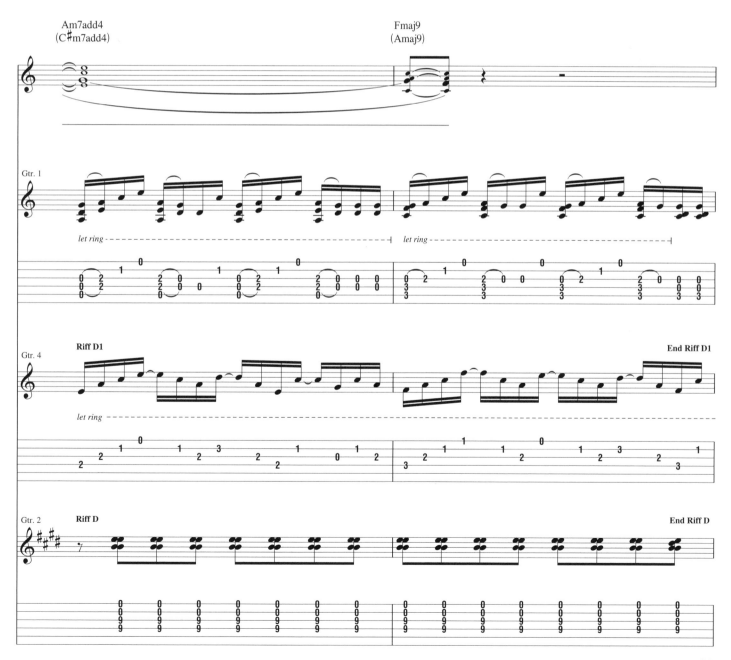

Am7add4
(C#m7add4)

Fmaj9
(Amaj9)

Gtr. 1

let ring

Gtr. 4

Riff D1

End Riff D1

let ring

Gtr. 2

Riff D

End Riff D

*See top of first page of song for chord diagrams pertaining to rhythm slashes.

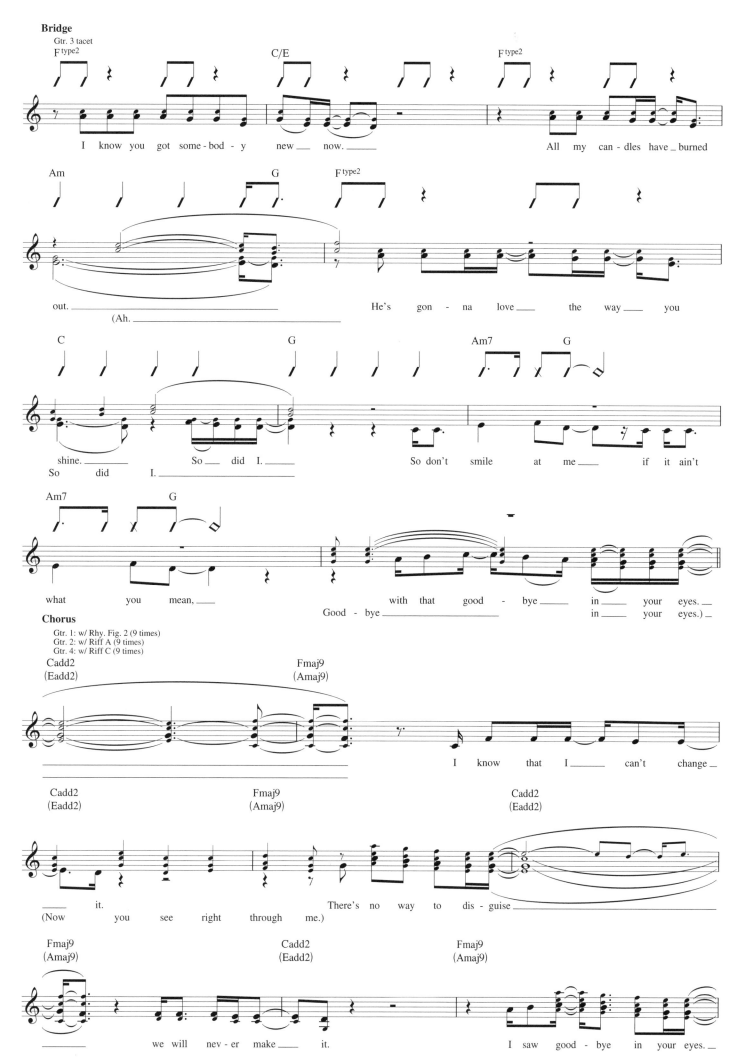

Outro

Gtr. 2: w/ Riff A (2 times)
Gtr. 4 tacet

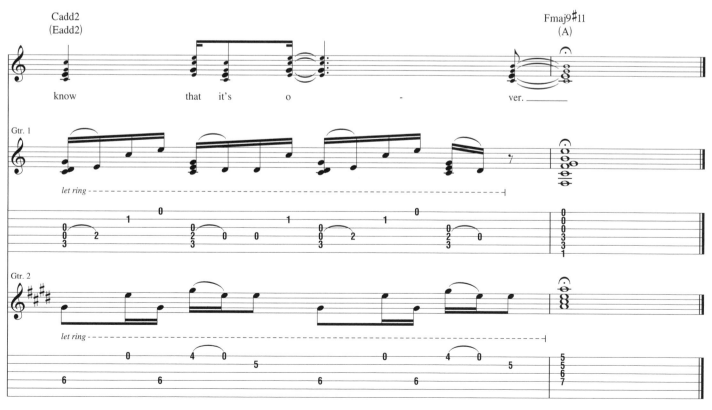

THE WIND

Words and Music by
Zac Brown, Wyatt Durrette,
Levi Lowrey and ZBB

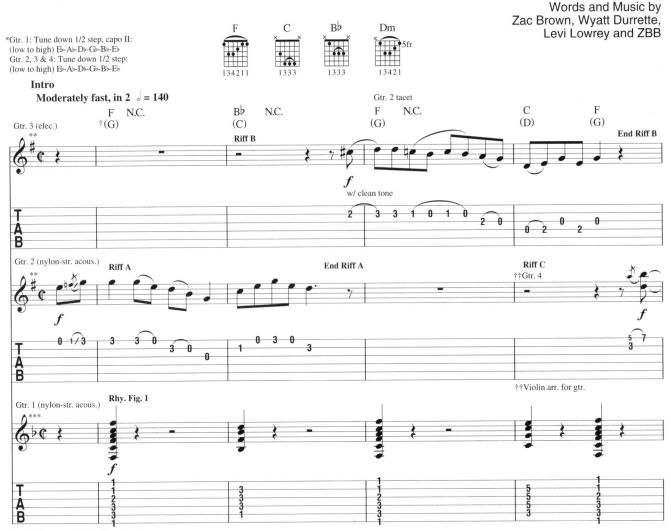

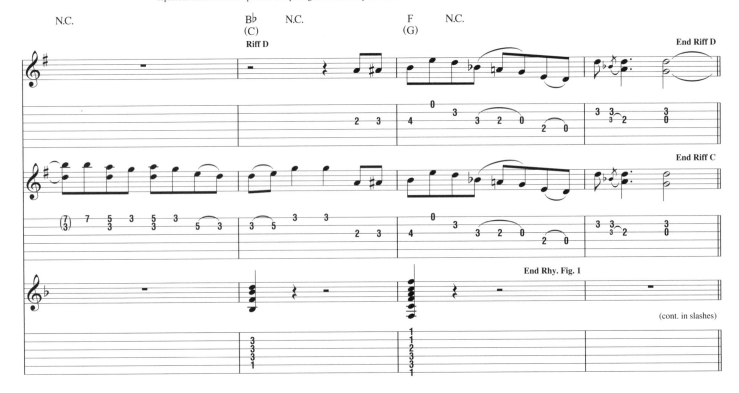

Verse

1. Thir-ty thou-sand feet a-bove the cit-y where I fell in love with you.
look like a coun-try sky; we're star-ing at the stars turned up-side

*Unless otherwise indicated, play only lowest note of chord on 1st and 3rd slash of each bar.

**See top of first page of song for chord diagrams pertaining to rhythm slashes.

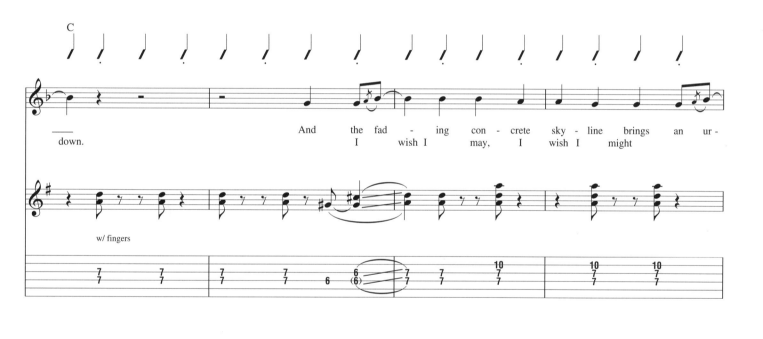

And the fad-ing con-crete sky-line brings an ur-
down. I wish I may, I wish I might

w/ fingers

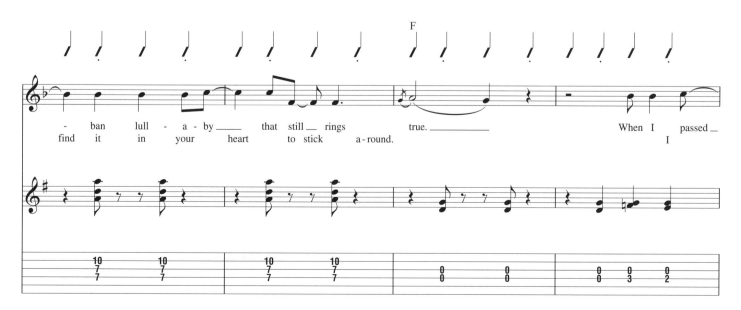

-ban lull-a-by that still rings true. When I passed
find it in your heart to stick a-round. I

you on the street ___ that day, should -a let that red scarf fly a - way ___ like

hate it had to end ___ this way; to - mor - row is a brand - new day. And the

an - y chance ___ I had of keep - ing you. ___

chanc - es here at love are pre - cious few

Like the north -

if

- ern wind a - blow - in', yeah, my lone - ly heart is fro - zen. Nev - er knew ___

some - one's out there wait - ing for a sweet ___ good - tim - in' la - dy to make you smile ___

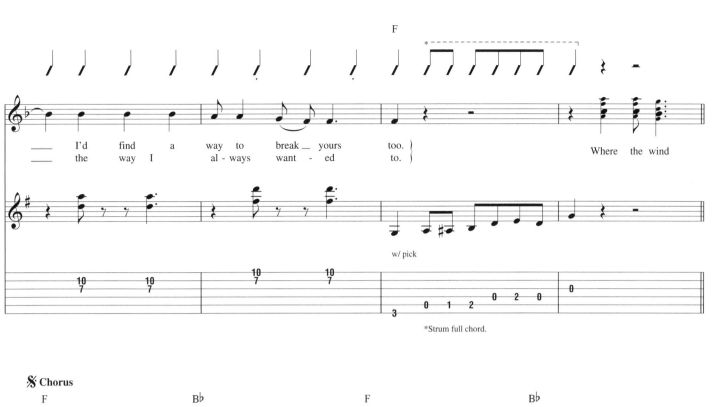

*Strum full chord.

ᛊ Chorus

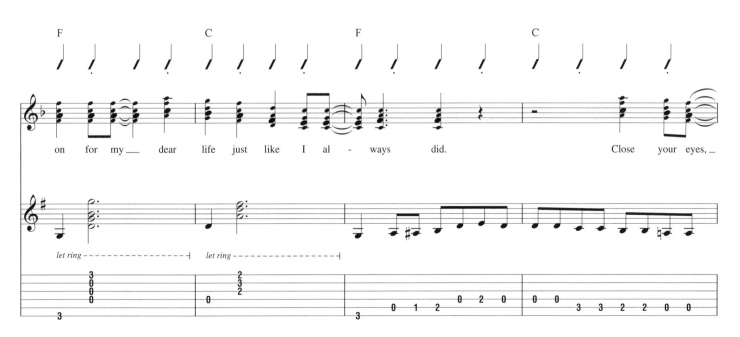

34

*Chord symbols reflect overall harmony.

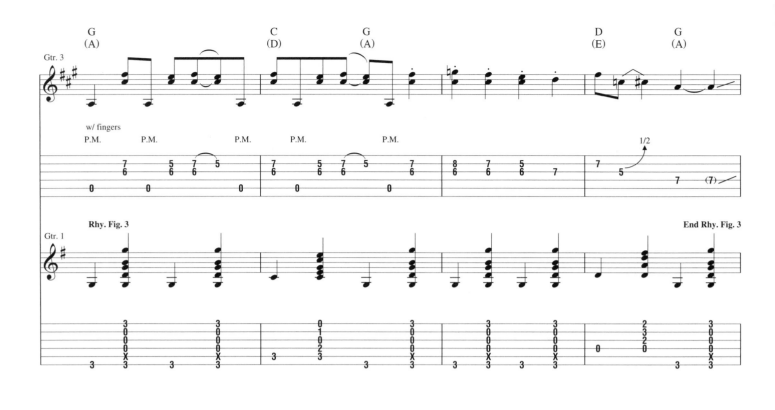

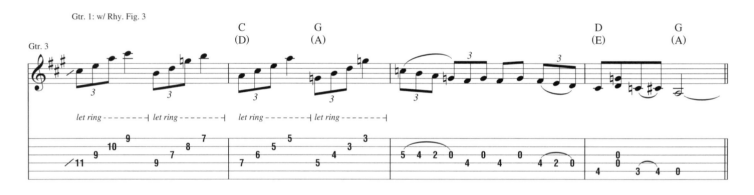

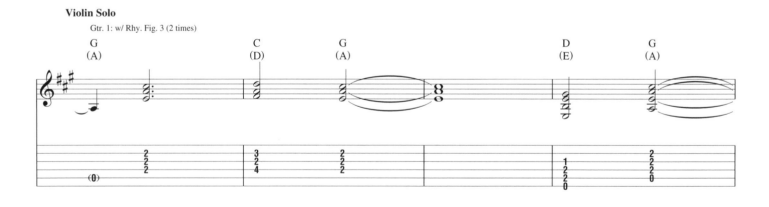

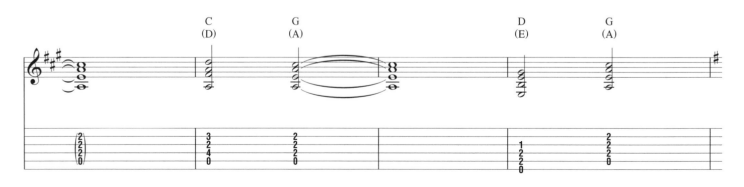

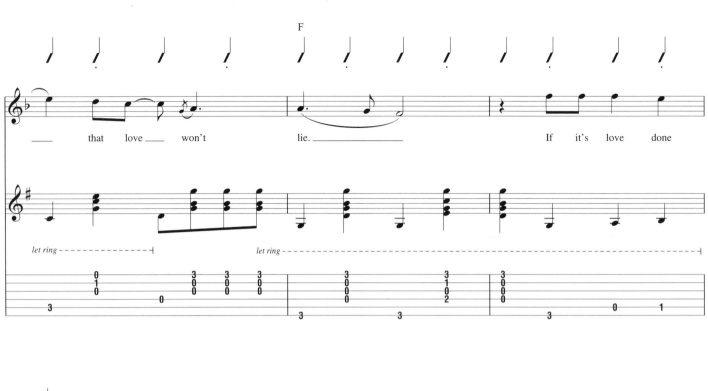

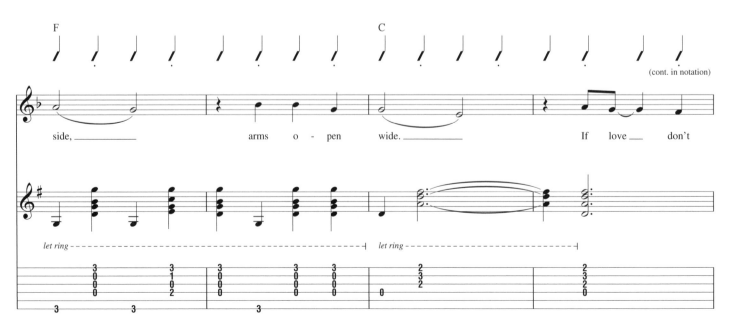

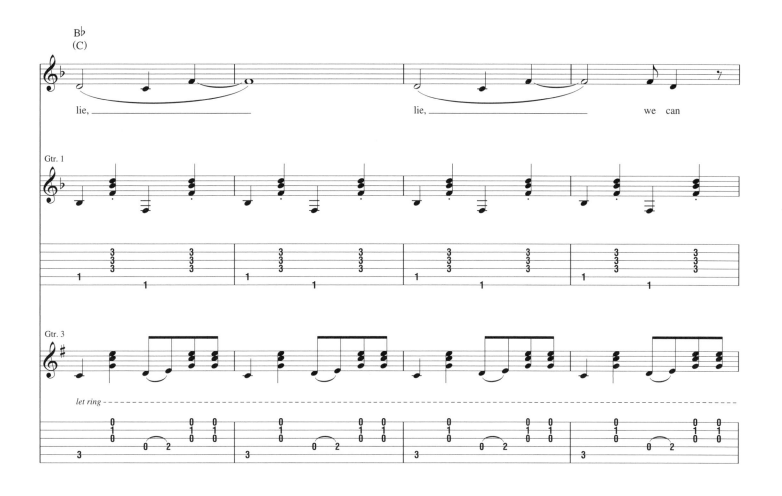

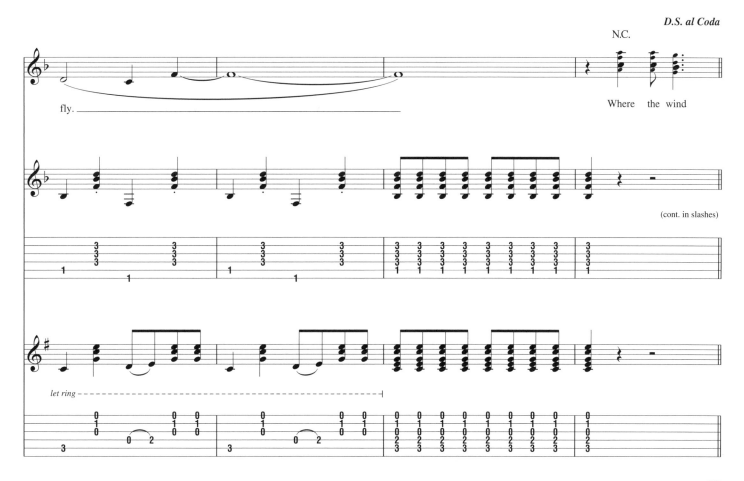

ISLAND SONG

Words and Music by
Nic Cowan

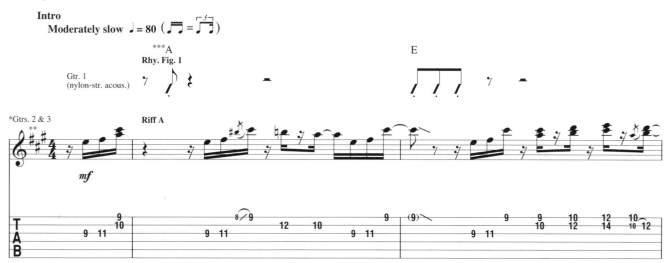

Tune down 1/2 step:
(low to high) E♭-A♭-D♭-G♭-B♭-E♭

Intro
Moderately slow ♩ = 80

Gtr. 1
(nylon-str. acous.)

*Gtrs. 2 & 3

*Two gtrs. arr for one. Gtr. 2: uke arr. for gtr.; Gtr. 3: elec. w/ slight dist.

**All music sounds 1/2 step lower than indicated due to tuning.

***See top of page for chord diagrams pertaining to rhythm slashes.

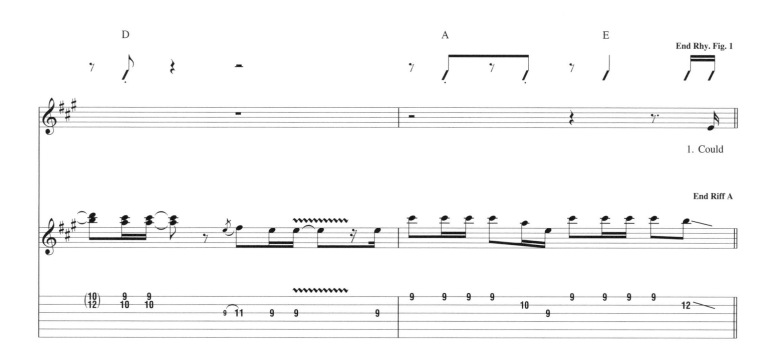

1. Could

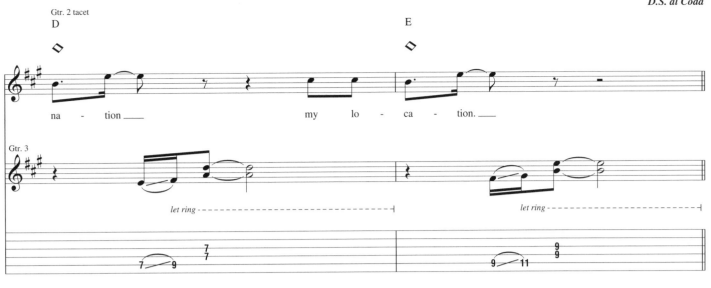

na - tion _____ my lo - ca - tion. _____

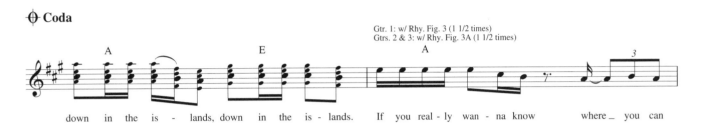

Coda

Gtr. 1: w/ Rhy. Fig. 3 (1 1/2 times)
Gtrs. 2 & 3: w/ Rhy. Fig. 3A (1 1/2 times)

down in the is - lands, down in the is - lands. If you real - ly wan - na know where _ you can

find me, _____ I'll be un - wind - ing _____ down, _ down, _ down, down, down in the is - lands.
(Down in the is - lands, down in the is - lands.)

You should _ lose track of your tim - ing, _____ grab a drink be -

Slower

side me _____ down in the is - lands, down in the is - is - lands.

SWEET ANNIE

Words and Music by
Zac Brown, Wyatt Durrette,
Sonia Leigh and John Pierce

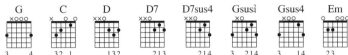

Gtr. 1: Tune down 1/2 step:
(low to high) Eb-Ab-Db-Gb-Bb-Eb
Gtr. 2: Open E tuning, down 1/2 step:
(low to high) Eb-Bb-Eb-G-Bb-Eb

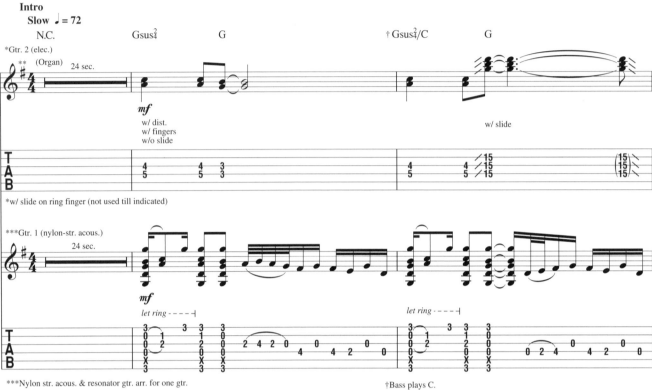

*w/ slide on ring finger (not used till indicated)

***Nylon str. acous. & resonator gtr. arr. for one gtr.

**All music sounds 1/2 step lower than indicated due to tunings.

†Bass plays C.

1. I been

(cont. in slashes)

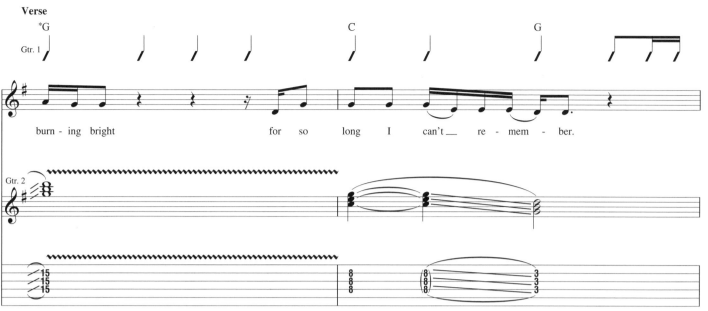

burn - ing bright   for so   long I   can't __ re - mem - ber.

*See top of first page of song for chord diagrams pertaining to rhythm slashes.

Pret - ty girls   and late - night bars __ seem to   be   my line of work.

**Fret this note behind slide w/ index finger.

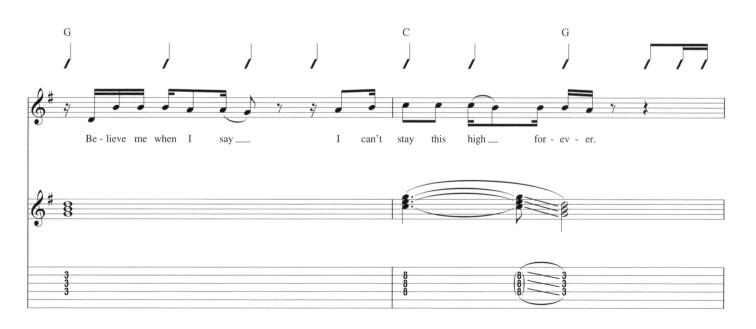

Be - lieve me when I   say __   I   can't stay this high __ for - ev - er.

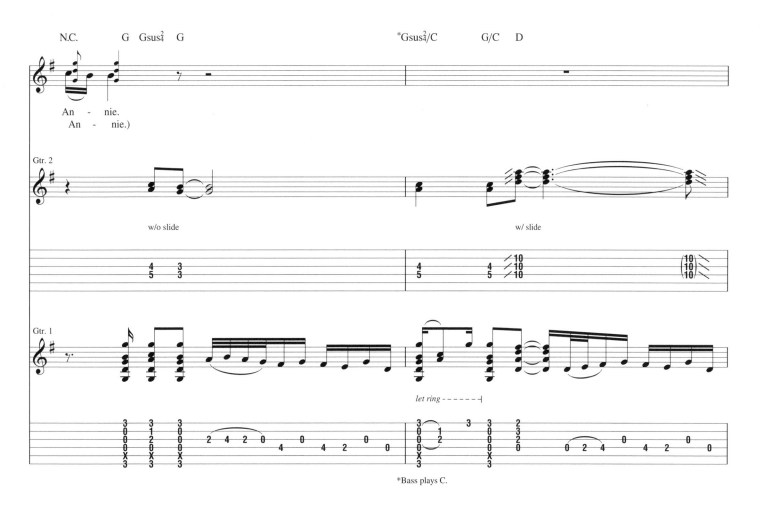

*Bass plays C.

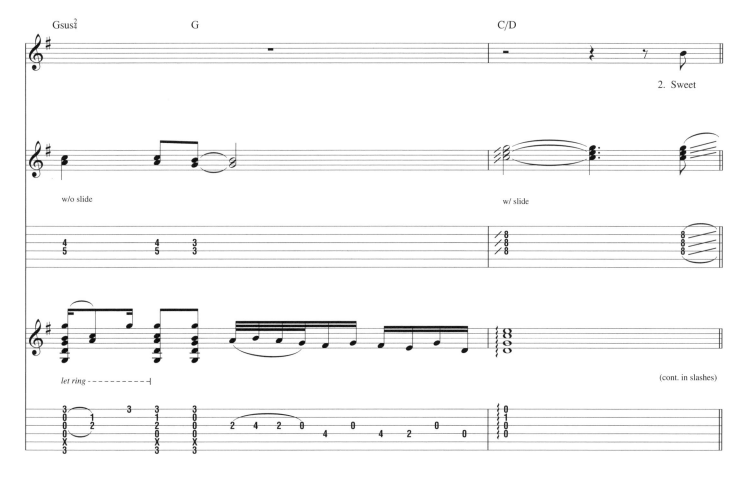

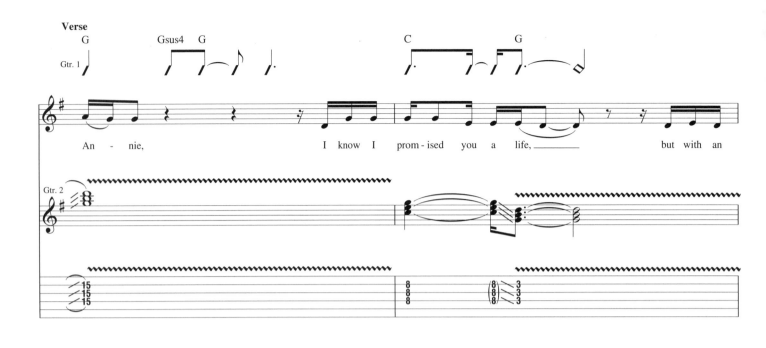

Verse

An - nie, I know I prom - ised you a life, _____ but with an

emp - ty bed _____ and the words _____ I said _____ don't car - ry an - y weight.

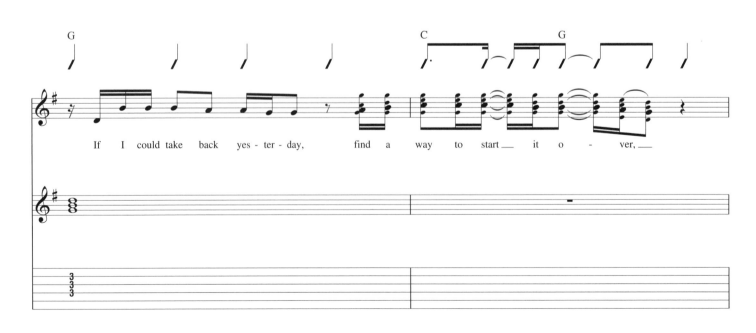

If I could take back yes - ter - day, find a way to start _____ it o - ver, _____

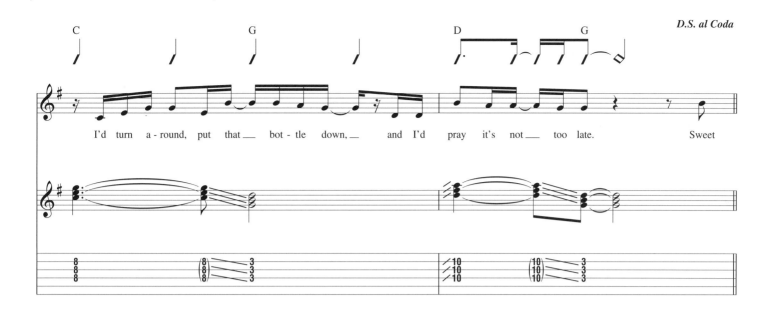

I'd turn a - round, put that __ bot - tle down, __ and I'd pray it's not __ too late. Sweet

⊕ Coda

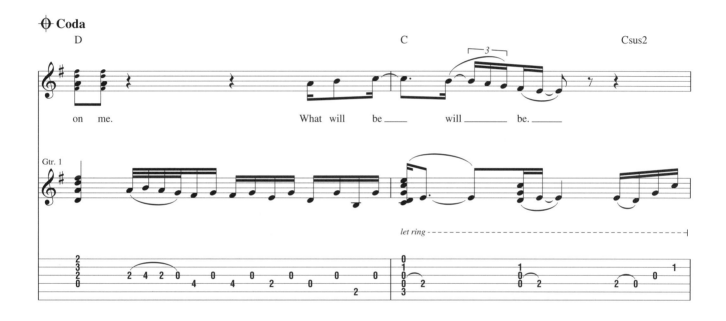

on me.   What will be __ will __ be. __

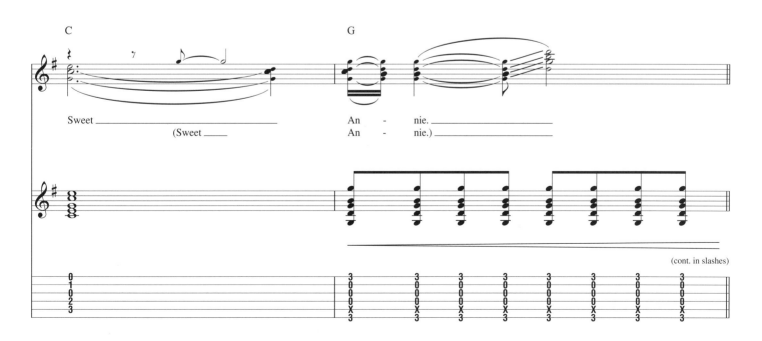

Sweet _____
(Sweet _____)

An - nie. _____
An - nie.) _____

Bridge

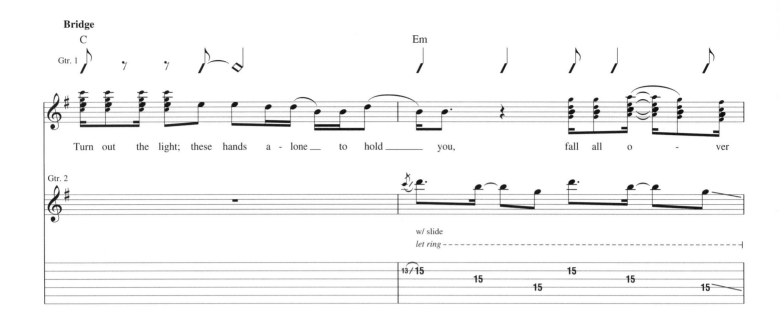

Turn out the light; these hands a - lone __ to hold __ you, fall all o - ver

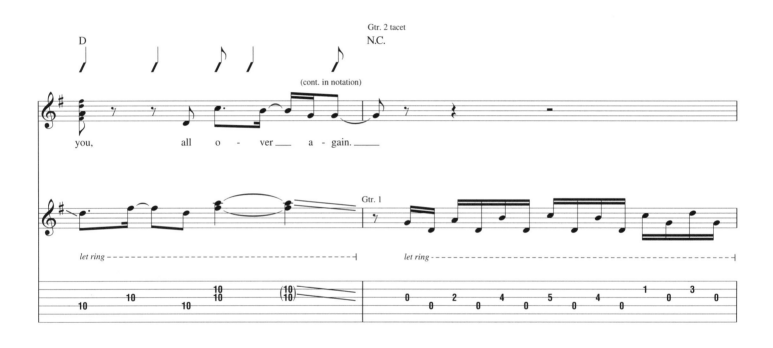

you, all o - ver __ a - gain. __

Come a lit - tle clos - er so I __ could show __ you my heart still beats __ fast for __

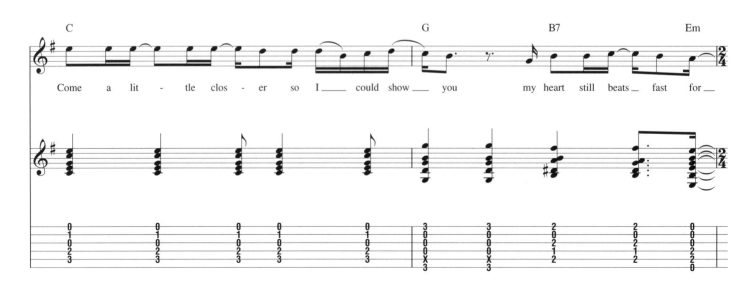

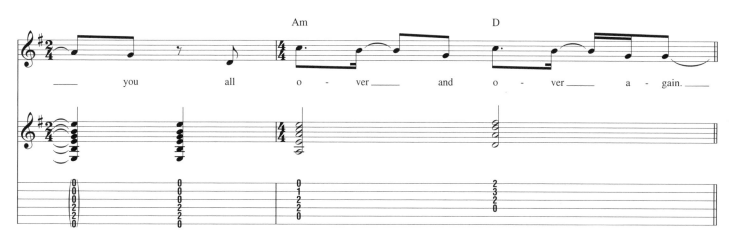

you   all   o - ver ___ and   o - ver ___ a - gain. ___

Interlude

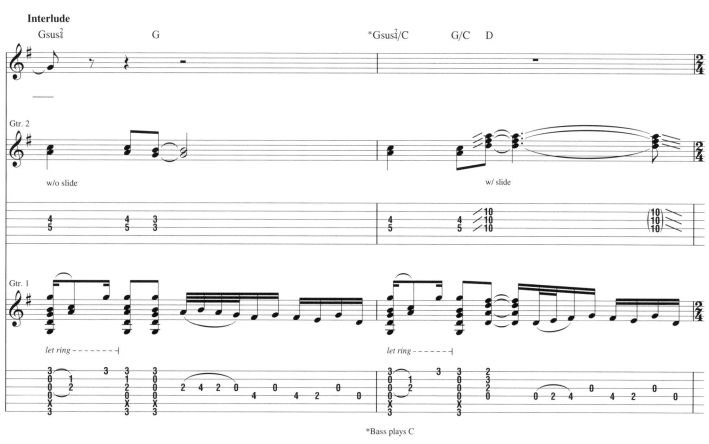

*Bass plays C

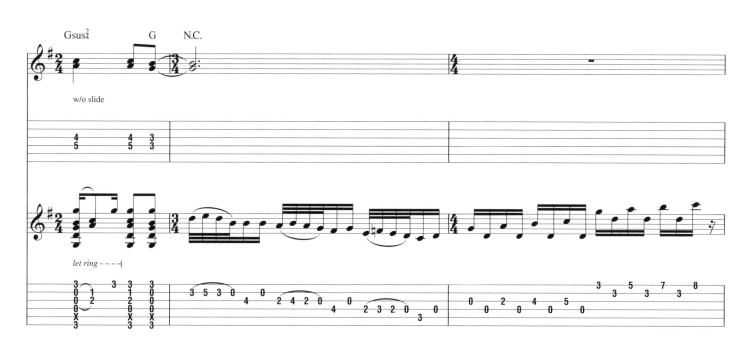

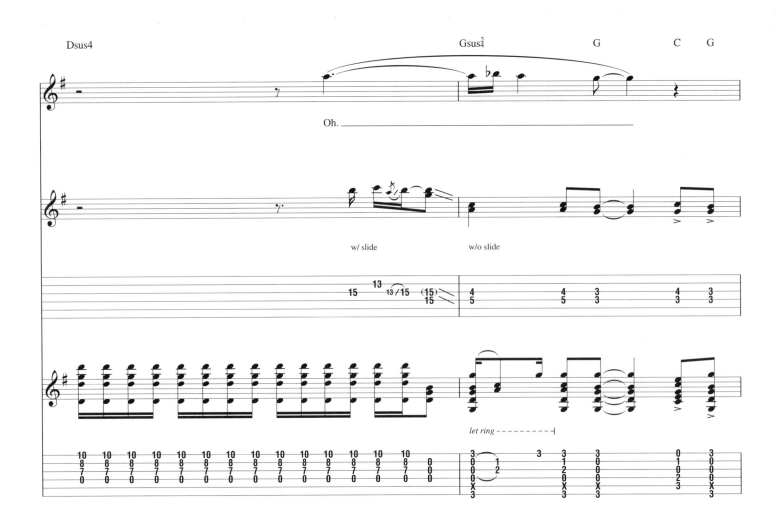

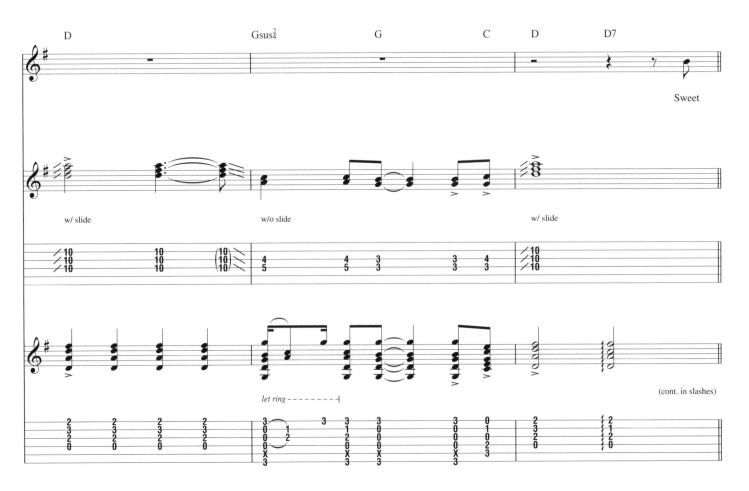

NATURAL DISASTER

Words and Music by
Zac Brown, Wyatt Durrette
and ZBB

Tune down 1/2 step:
(low to high) Eb-Ab-Db-Gb-Bb-Eb

Intro
Moderately slow ♩ = 76

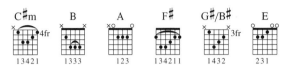

E
(Organ)

*All music sounds 1/2 step lower than indicated due to tuning.
**Chord symbols reflect overall harmony.

Had lips like _ can-dy, hair float-ed like

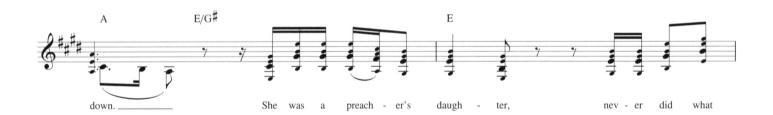

wa - ter. Skin like vel - vet made the whole damn world _____ slow

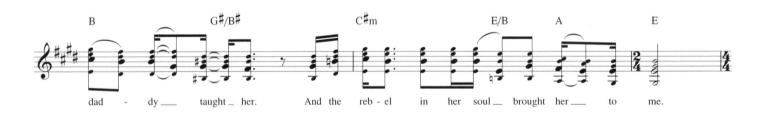

down. _____ She was a preach - er's daugh - ter, nev - er did what

dad - dy _ taught _ her. And the reb - el in her soul _ brought her _ to me.

Double time ♩ = 152

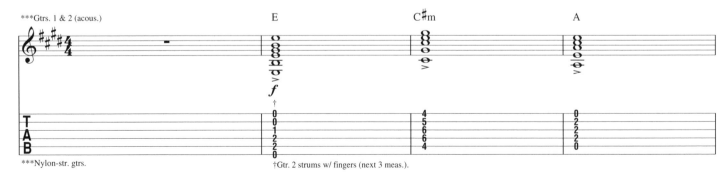

***Gtrs. 1 & 2 (acous.)

***Nylon-str. gtrs.   †Gtr. 2 strums w/ fingers (next 3 meas.).

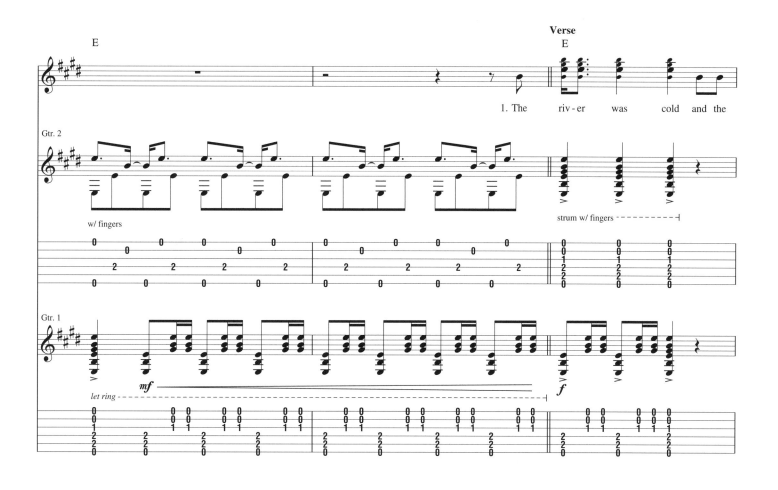

Verse

1. The riv-er was cold and the

riv-er was wide. She flowed from the moun-tain straight a-

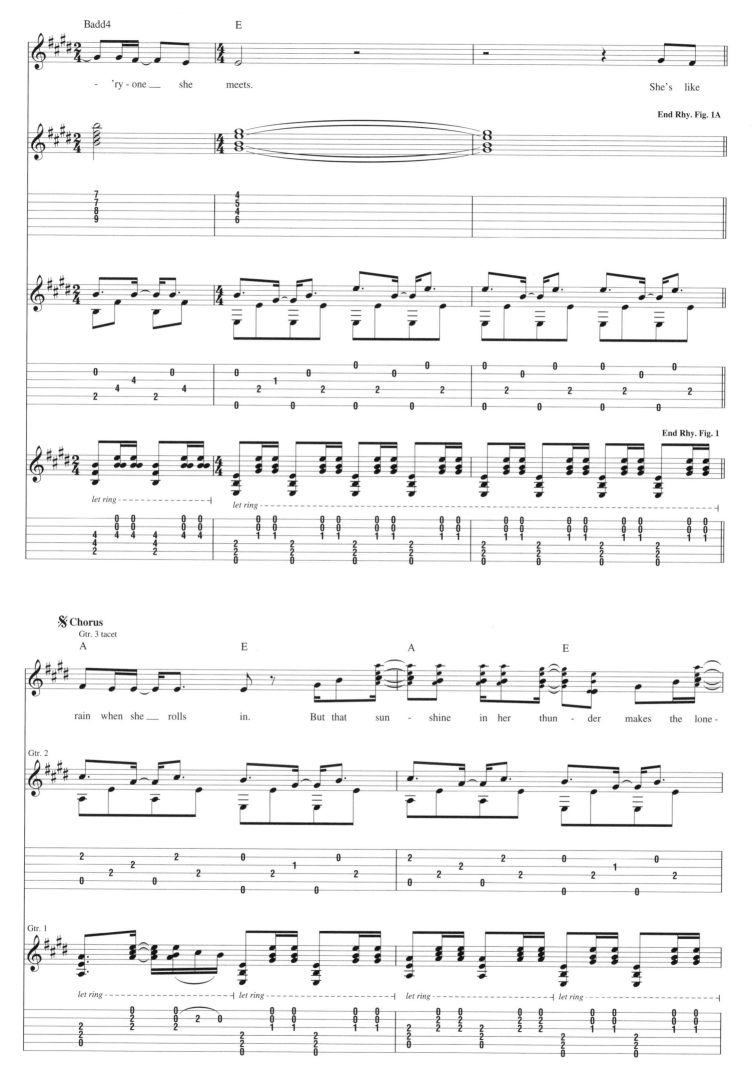

-li-est ___ heart won-der if the ride ___ is worth the pain. ___ Might not be ___

___ storm clouds in-side. Oh, but don't ___ you wor-ry, friend. She's

60

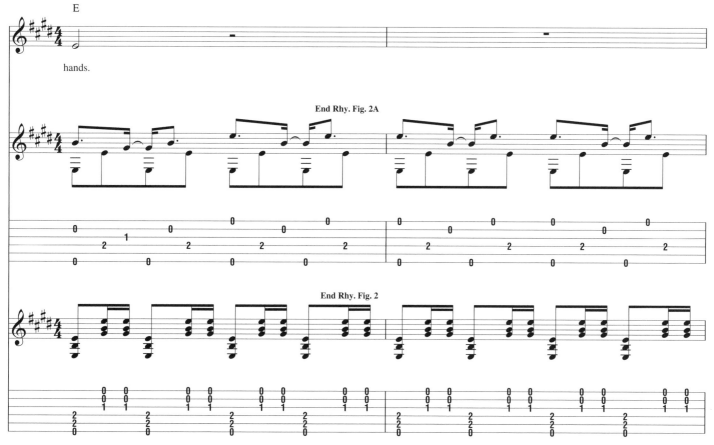

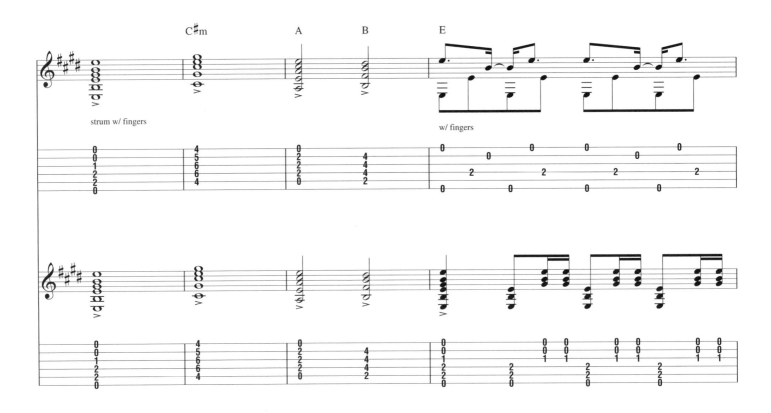

Verse

E

2. Lord, please know it's not

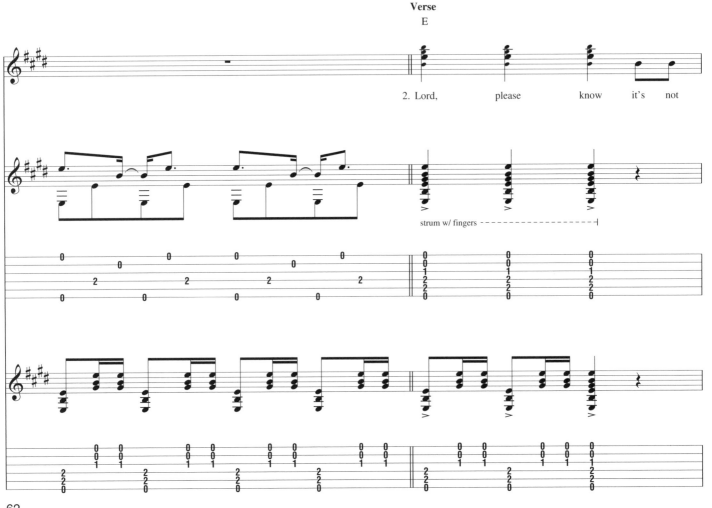

Interlude

Gtr. 1: w/ Rhy. Fig. 2 (4th meas.)

**See top of first page of song for chord diagrams pertaining to rhythm slashes.

Gtrs. 3 & 4 tacet

nat - u - ral ___ dis - as - ter; she'll tear the land ___ in two. She's

Gtr. 2

*For next 11 meas., play only lowest note of chord on downbeats; play full chord on upbeats. Pick w/ all downstrokes.

run - ning to ___ be run - ning 'cause it's all ___ she knows to do. She's a

tum - ble - weed ___ a roll - ing, (a) riv - er run - ning wild, ___ (a)

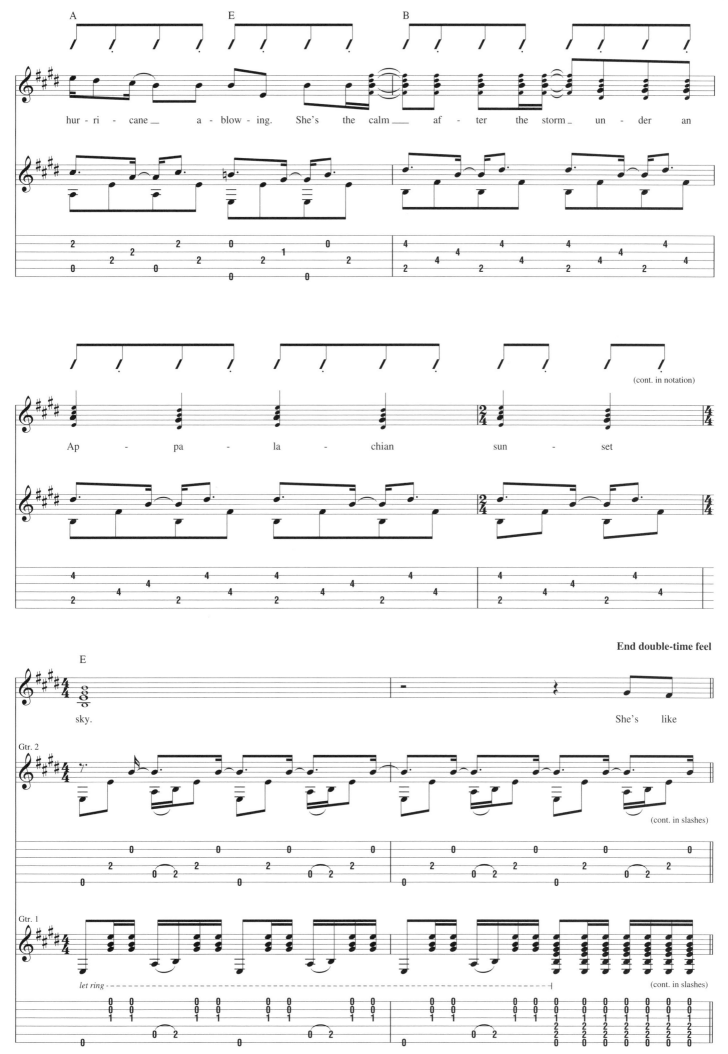

Breakdown-Chorus

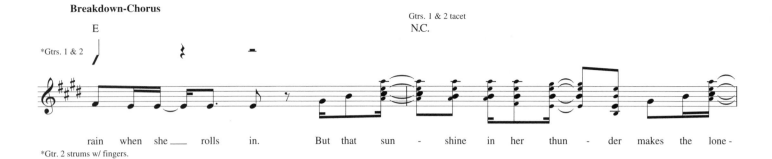

rain when she ___ rolls in. But that sun - shine in her thun - der makes the lone -

- li - est ___ heart won - der if the ride ___ is worth the pain. ___ Might not be

___ storm clouds in - side. Oh, but don't ___ you wor - ry, friend. She's

com - ing 'round the bend; ___ she's hold - ing light - ning in ___ both ___ hands. She's like

Outro

rain; she rolls in. ___ But there's

68

OVERNIGHT

Words and Music by
Zac Brown and Nic Cowan

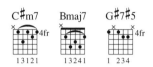

Tune down 1/2 step:
(low to high) E♭-A♭-D♭-G♭-B♭-E♭

Verse

Moderately slow ♩ = 92

*All music sounds 1/2 step lower than indicated due to tuning.

1. I don't know how _ much more _ of this _ that I

_ can _ take. _ I want _ you, and

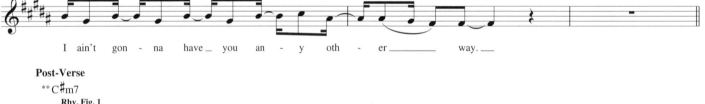

I ain't gon - na have _ you an - y oth - er _ way. _

Post-Verse

**C#m7

Rhy. Fig. 1

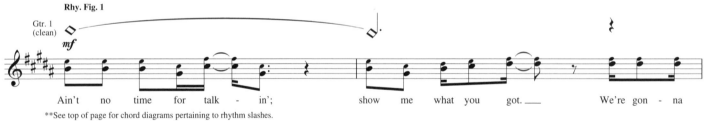

Ain't no time for talk - in'; show me what you got. _ We're gon - na

*See top of page for chord diagrams pertaining to rhythm slashes.

Bmaj7

End Rhy. Fig. 1

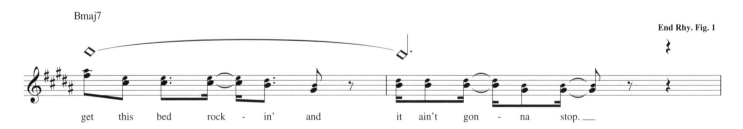

get this bed rock - in' and it ain't gon - na stop. _

C#m7

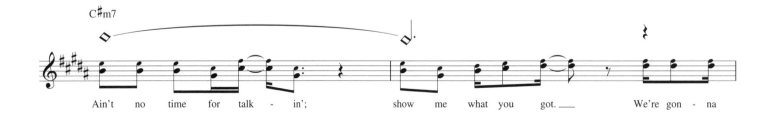

Ain't no time for talk - in'; show me what you got. _ We're gon - na

I'm your judge and ju - ry, so you got - ta do the time. O - ver -

Chorus

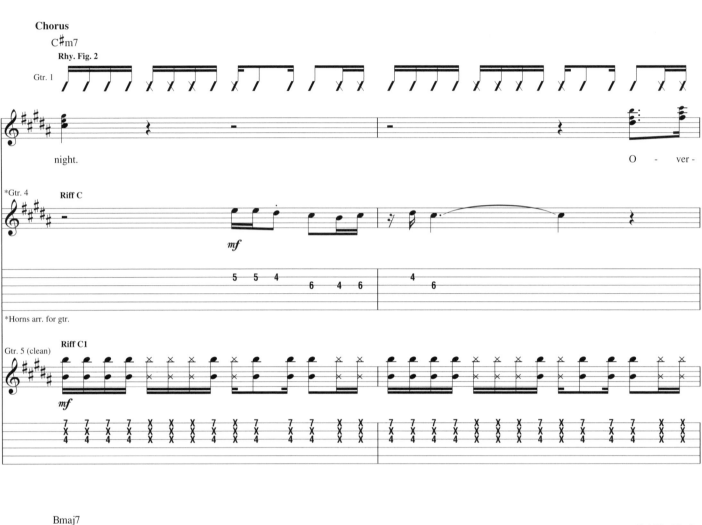

night.

O - ver -

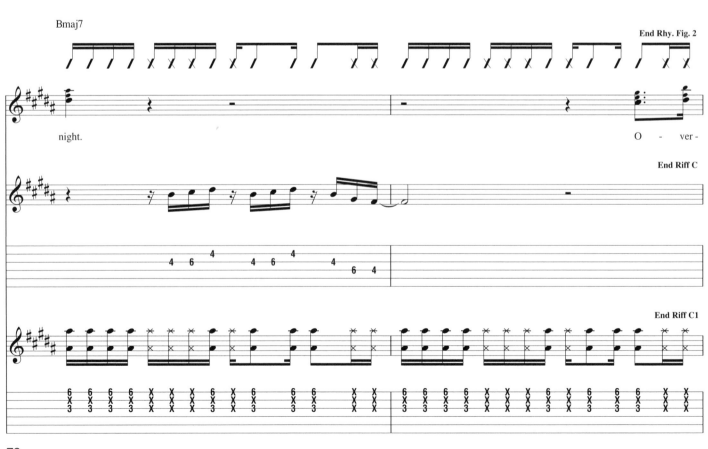

night.

O - ver -

I got-ta make sure ___ you ain't hid-in' noth-in' no-

Bmaj7

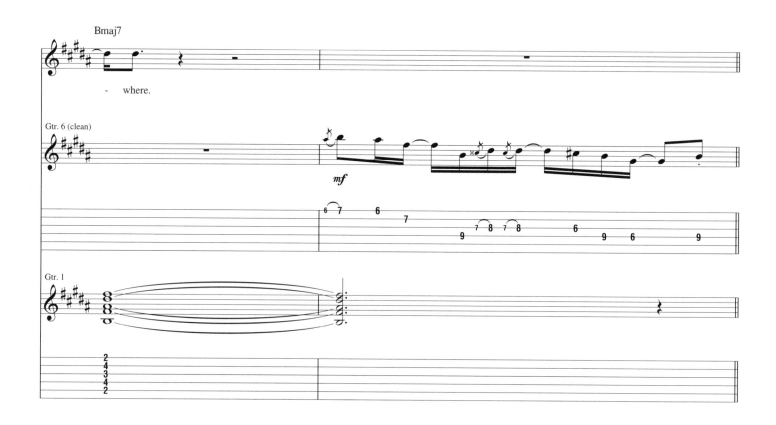

- where.

Gtr. 6 (clean)

Gtr. 1

Post-Verse

Gtr. 6 tacet

C#m7

Ain't no time for talk-in'; show me what you got. ___ We're gon-na

Gtr. 1

*Chord symbols reflect overall harmony (next 8 meas.).

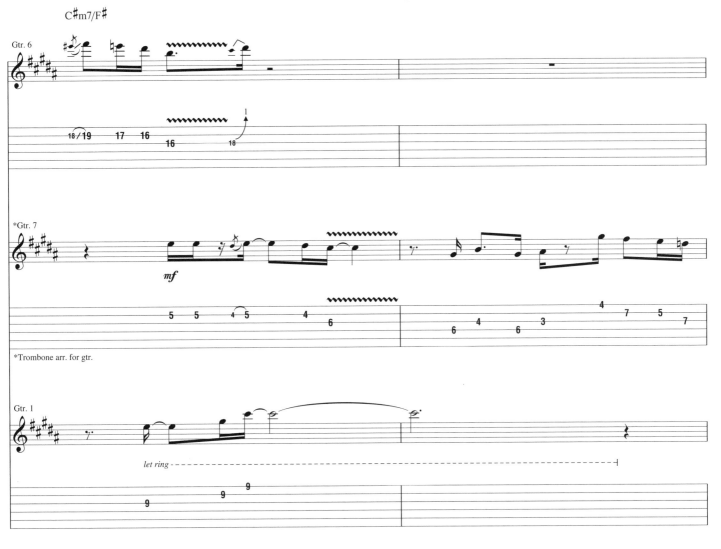

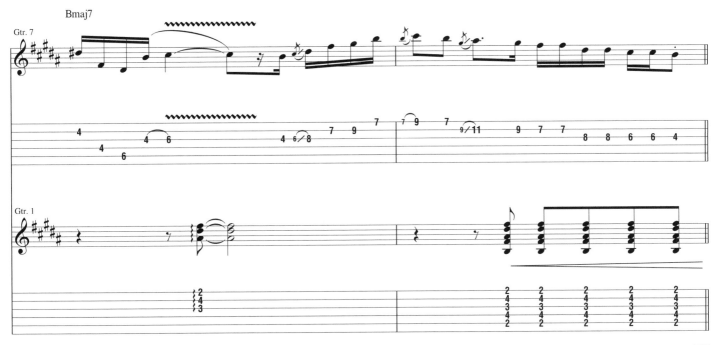

LANCE'S SONG

Words and Music by
Zac Brown and Nic Cowan

*Gtr. 1: Tune down 1/2 step, capo IV:
(low to high) E♭-A♭-D♭-G♭-B♭-E♭
Gtr. 2: Open E tuning, down 1/2 step:
(low to high) E♭-B♭-E♭-G-B♭-E♭
Gtrs. 3 & 4: Tune down 1/2 step:
(low to high) E♭-A♭-D♭-G♭-B♭-E♭

Intro
Moderately slow, in 2 ♩ = 80

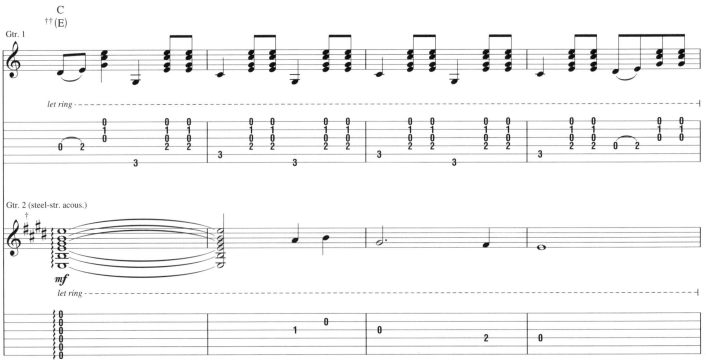

*Equivalent to standard tuning, capo III.

　**Music for capoed gtr. & vocal sounds a minor 3rd higher than indicated due to capo & tuning. Capoed fret is "0" in tab.

　***Chord symbols reflect basic harmony.

†Music for non-capoed gtrs. sounds 1/2 step lower than indicated due to tuning.

　††Symbols in parentheses represent chord names respective to non-capoed gtrs. Symbols above represent chord names respective to capoed gtr. & vocal.

C
(E)

End Riff A

End Riff A1

End Rhy. Fig. 1

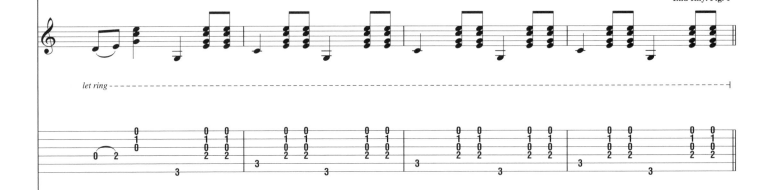

End Rhy. Fig. 2

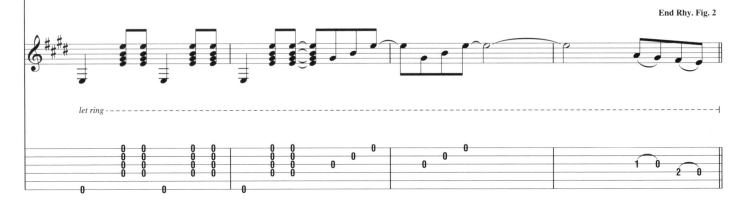

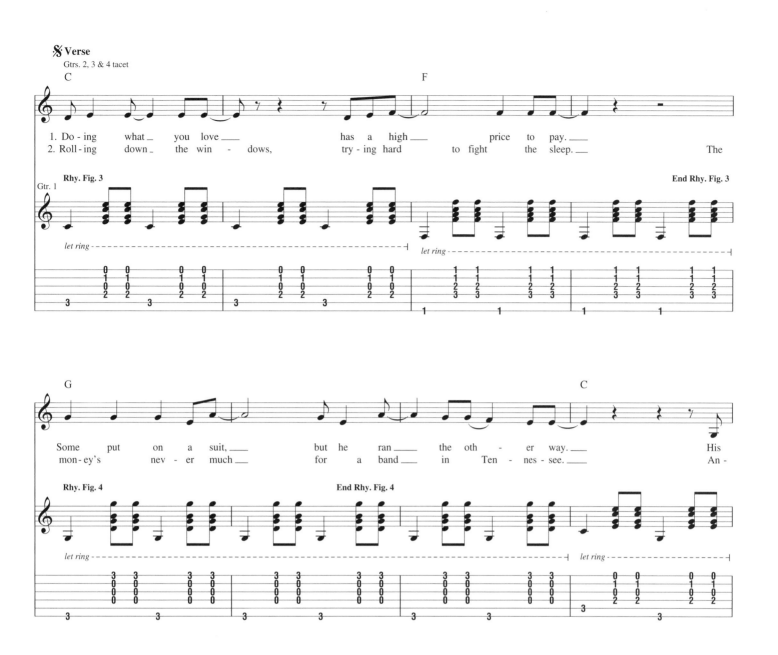

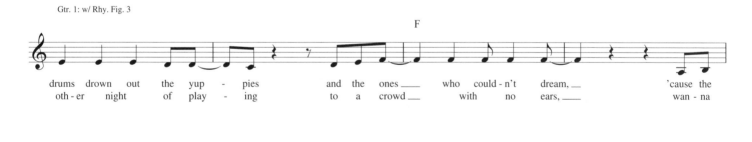

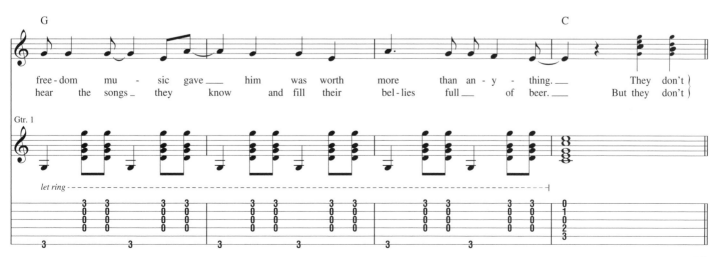

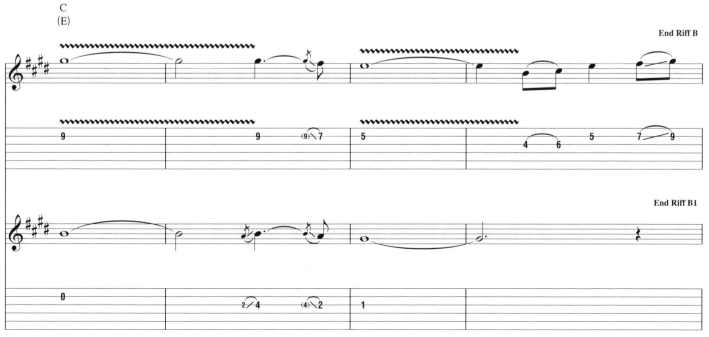

when the thun-der comes, ___ you can hear ___ his kick ___ drum ___ in the

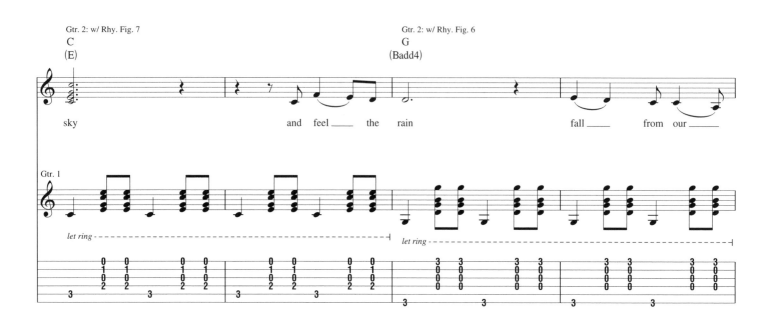

sky ___ and feel ___ the rain ___ fall ___ from our ___

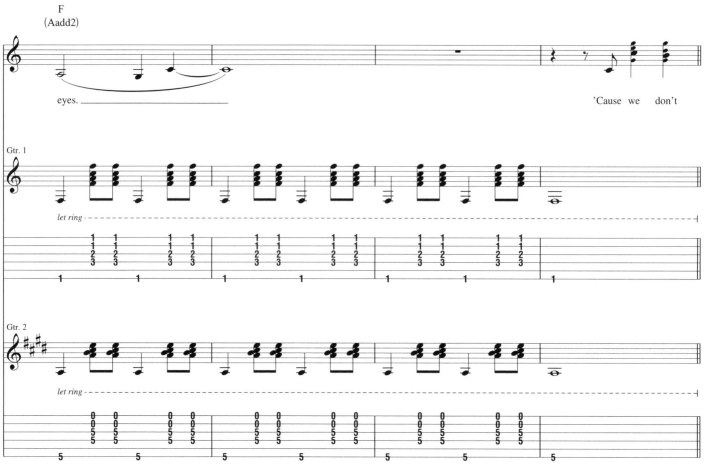

eyes. _____ 'Cause we don't

DAY THAT I DIE

Words and Music by
Zac Brown, Wyatt Durrette
and Nic Cowan

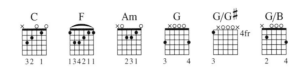

*Gtrs. 1 & 3: Tune down 1/2 step, capo IV:
(low to high) E♭-A♭-D♭-G♭-B♭-E♭
Gtrs. 2 & 4: Tune down 1/2 step:
(low to high) E♭-A♭-D♭-G♭-B♭-E♭

Intro
Moderately slow ♩ = 80

**Violin & organ arr. for gtr.
***Music for non-capoed gtrs. sounds 1/2 step lower than indicated due to tuning.

*Equivalent to standard tuning, capo III
†Music for capoed gtrs. sounds a minor 3rd higher than indicated due to capo & tuning.
††Symbols in parentheses represent chord names respective to non-capoed gtrs.
Symbols above represent chord names respective to capoed gtrs. & vocal. Capoed fret is "0" in tab.

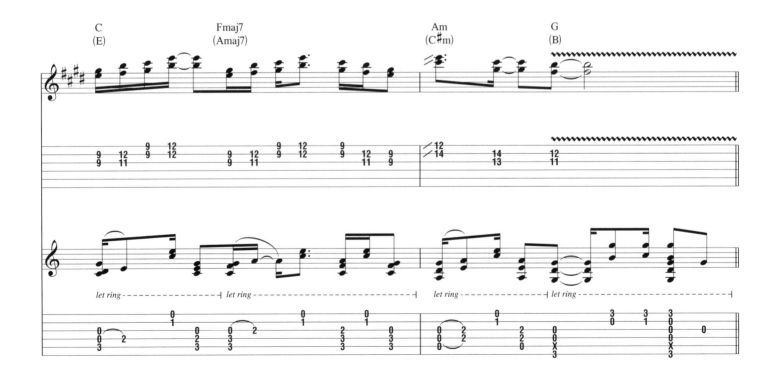

Verse

Gtr. 1: w/ Rhy. Fig. 1 (4 times)
1st time, Gtr. 2 tacet
2nd time, Gtr. 3 tacet
2nd time, Gtr. 4: w/ Rhy. Fill 1

Zac Brown: 1. Ear - ly morn - ing in a mo - tel ____ room, sun - shine try'n' to creep on through. ___
Amos Lee: 2. A part of dawn to be a - shamed ___ of, good peo - ple aren't sup - posed to be up. ___

Lost sleep but I found a tune ____ stuck in - side ____ my head. ___
I found peace with this path I took, as I lay down ___ my head. ___

Cig - a - rettes and tank of gas, ____ head - ed off to no - where fast. ___
Cross - roads, you got - ta choose ____ which way; do we win or lose? ___

Got - ta find a way to make this feel - ing ____ last. ____ 'Cause I be -
And ev - 'ry bone in my soul says I sing on ____ to. I be -

Pre-Chorus

C   F   Am   G

Gtr. 1

lieve that I ____ was born with a song ___ in - side of me. ___ Nev - er
lieve that I ____ was born with a song ___ in - side of me. ___ Nev - er

*Gtr. 3 (elec.)

mf
w/ clean tone
let ring - - - - - - - - - - - - - - - - -   *let ring -*

*Two gtrs. arr. for one
**See top of first page of song for chord diagrams pertaining to rhythm slashes.

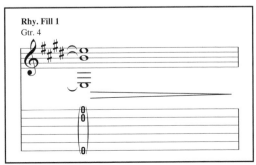

Rhy. Fill 1
Gtr. 4

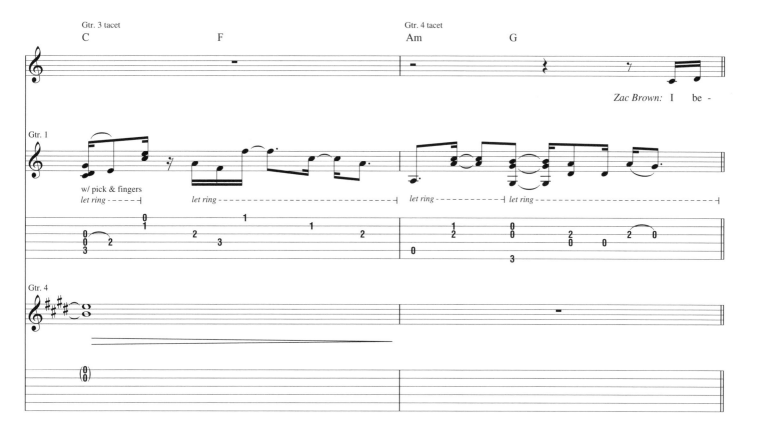

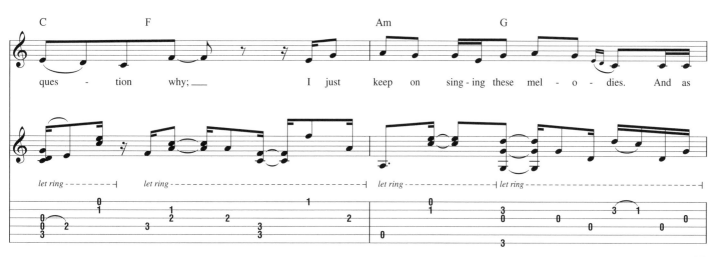

LAST BUT NOT LEAST

Words and Music by
Zac Brown, Wyatt Durrette,
Mac McAnally, Jimmy De Martini
and Coy Bowles

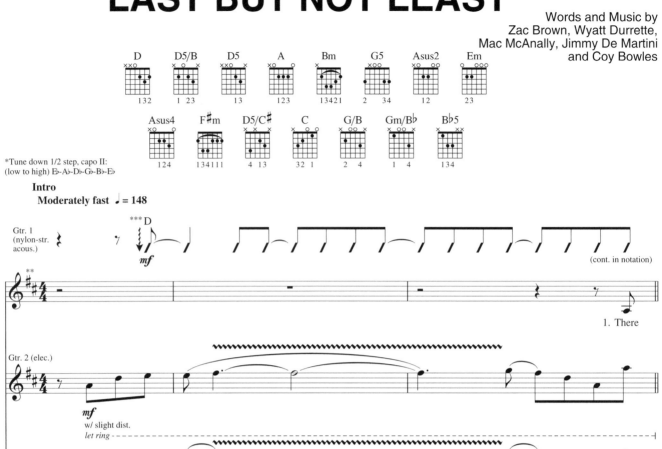

*Tune down 1/2 step, capo II:
(low to high) E♭-A♭-D♭-G♭-B♭-E♭

Intro
Moderately fast ♩ = 148

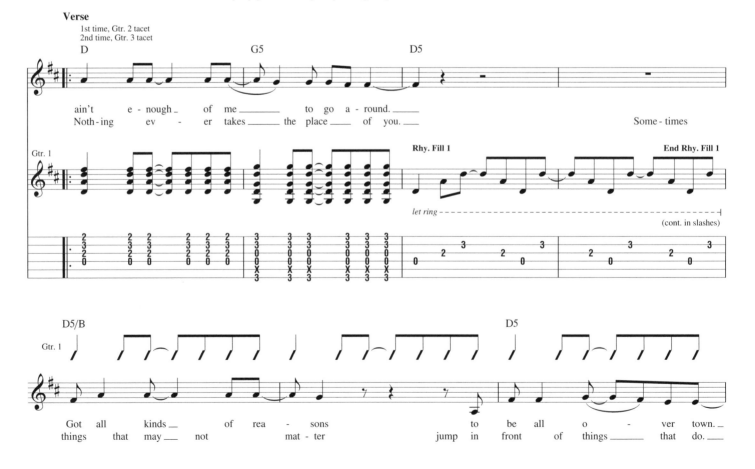

*Equivalent to standard tuning, capo I

**All music sounds 1/2 higher than indicated due to capo & tuning. Capoed fret is "0" in tab.

***See top of page for chord diagrams pertaining to rhythm slashes.

Verse

1st time, Gtr. 2 tacet
2nd time, Gtr. 3 tacet

ain't e - nough ___ of me _____ to go a - round. _____
Noth - ing ev - er takes _____ the place _____ of you. _____ Some - times

Got all kinds ___ of rea - sons to be all o - ver town. ___
things that may ___ not mat - ter jump in front of things ___ that do. ___

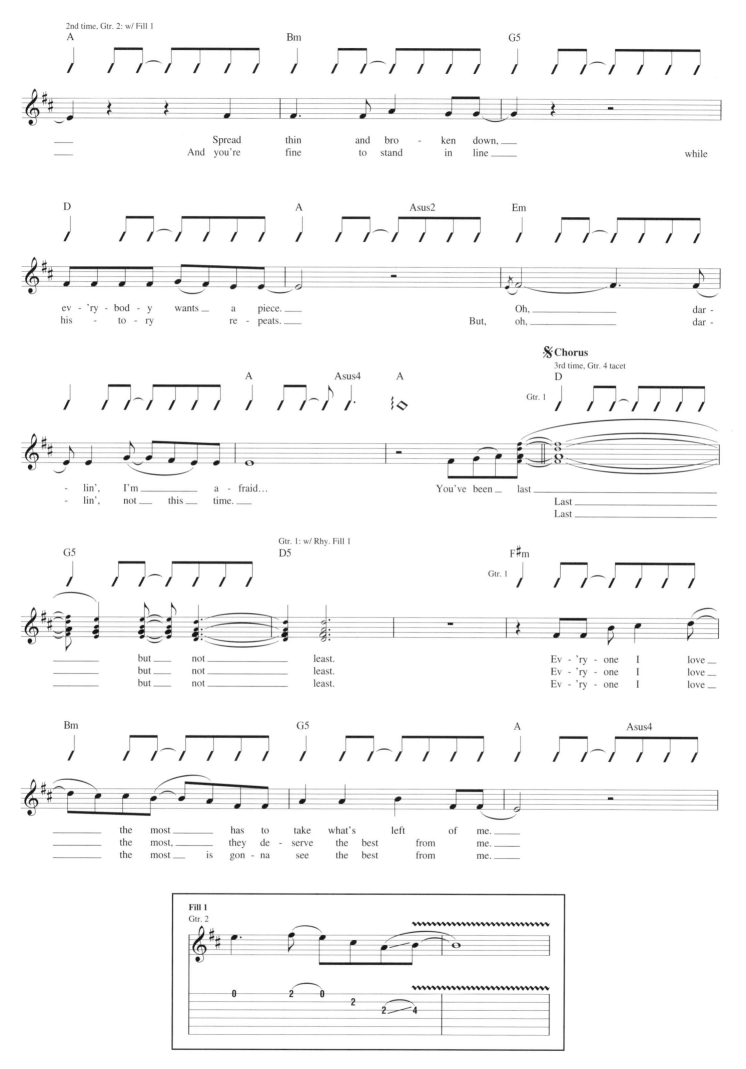

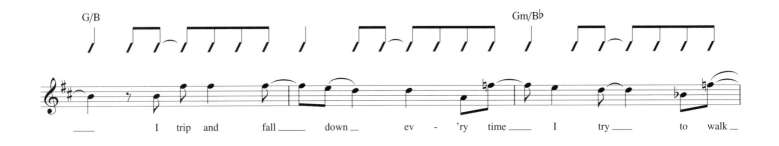

_I trip and fall___ down___ ev - 'ry time___ I try___ to walk___

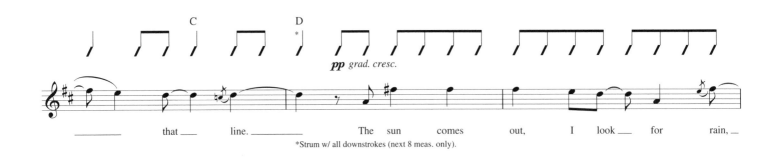

pp grad. cresc.

_____ that___ line._____ The sun comes out, I look___ for rain,___

*Strum w/ all downstrokes (next 8 meas. only).

_____ to search for joy___ and I____ find the pain. ____ I swear___

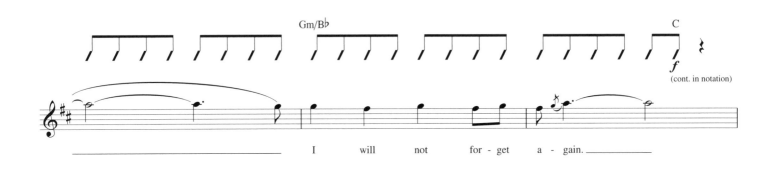

_f_

(cont. in notation)

_____ I will not for - get a - gain._____

Half-time feel

N.C.   D   C

Last _____   but ___ not _____   least. _____
(Last.) _____

Gtrs. 1 & 4

let ring -

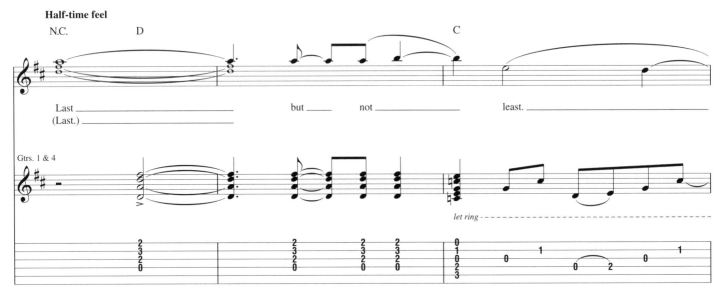

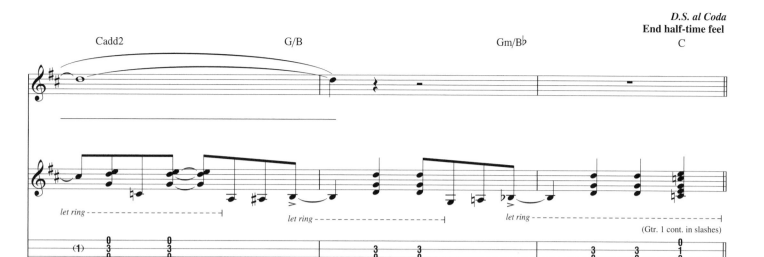

Coda

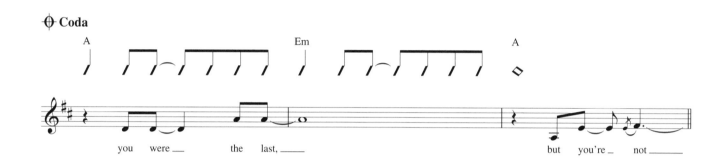

you were __ the last, ___ but you're __ not __

Outro

Gtr. 1: w/ Rhy. Fig. 1

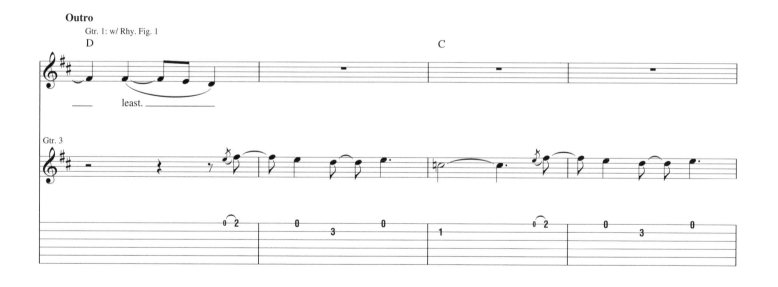

__ least. ___

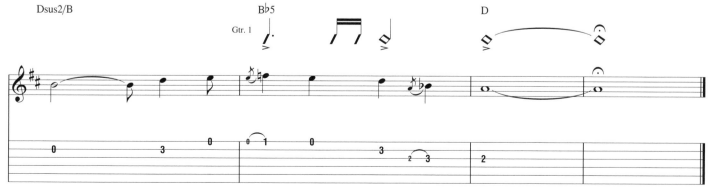

GUITAR NOTATION LEGEND

Guitar music can be notated three different ways: on a *musical staff*, in *tablature*, and in *rhythm slashes*.

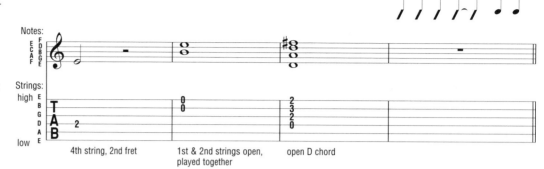

RHYTHM SLASHES are written above the staff. Strum chords in the rhythm indicated. Use the chord diagrams found at the top of the first page of the transcription for the appropriate chord voicings. Round noteheads indicate single notes.

THE MUSICAL STAFF shows pitches and rhythms and is divided by bar lines into measures. Pitches are named after the first seven letters of the alphabet.

TABLATURE graphically represents the guitar fingerboard. Each horizontal line represents a string, and each number represents a fret.

4th string, 2nd fret

1st & 2nd strings open, played together

open D chord

HALF-STEP BEND: Strike the note and bend up 1/2 step.

WHOLE-STEP BEND: Strike the note and bend up one step.

GRACE NOTE BEND: Strike the note and immediately bend up as indicated.

SLIGHT (MICROTONE) BEND: Strike the note and bend up 1/4 step.

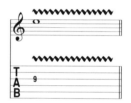

BEND AND RELEASE: Strike the note and bend up as indicated, then release back to the original note. Only the first note is struck.

PRE-BEND: Bend the note as indicated, then strike it.

VIBRATO: The string is vibrated by rapidly bending and releasing the note with the fretting hand.

WIDE VIBRATO: The pitch is varied to a greater degree by vibrating with the fretting hand.

HAMMER-ON: Strike the first (lower) note with one finger, then sound the higher note (on the same string) with another finger by fretting it without picking.

PULL-OFF: Place both fingers on the notes to be sounded. Strike the first note and without picking, pull the finger off to sound the second (lower) note.

LEGATO SLIDE: Strike the first note and then slide the same fret-hand finger up or down to the second note. The second note is not struck.

SHIFT SLIDE: Same as legato slide, except the second note is struck.

TRILL: Very rapidly alternate between the notes indicated by continuously hammering on and pulling off.

TAPPING: Hammer ("tap") the fret indicated with the pick-hand index or middle finger and pull off to the note fretted by the fret hand.

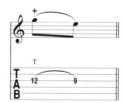

NATURAL HARMONIC: Strike the note while the fret-hand lightly touches the string directly over the fret indicated.

PINCH HARMONIC: The note is fretted normally and a harmonic is produced by adding the edge of the thumb or the tip of the index finger of the pick hand to the normal pick attack.

PICK SCRAPE: The edge of the pick is rubbed down (or up) the string, producing a scratchy sound.

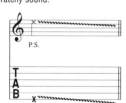

MUFFLED STRINGS: A percussive sound is produced by laying the fret hand across the string(s) without depressing, and striking them with the pick hand.

PALM MUTING: The note is partially muted by the pick hand lightly touching the string(s) just before the bridge.

RAKE: Drag the pick across the strings indicated with a single motion.

TREMOLO PICKING: The note is picked as rapidly and continuously as possible.

VIBRATO BAR DIVE AND RETURN: The pitch of the note or chord is dropped a specified number of steps (in rhythm), then returned to the original pitch.

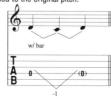

VIBRATO BAR SCOOP: Depress the bar just before striking the note, then quickly release the bar.

VIBRATO BAR DIP: Strike the note and then immediately drop a specified number of steps, then release back to the original pitch.

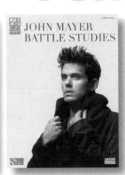